"Get this book and take it with you everywhere. And as you're riding a bus or eating your lunch, read it for 5 minutes (that's what it took me to read most of the essays). I'm pretty sure I can guarantee that you'll have the most spiritually fulfilling bus ride or lunch of your life."

>—Mark Massa, SJ
>Professor of Church History
>Boston College

"Bill Graham is a wonderfully natural writer, gifted with musically colloquial language, radiant good sense, and numerous insights, always freshly phrased, into the ways of the spirit. He is generous in his attitudes and imaginative in his use of passages from Scripture which enhance and support out lives. There is a living pulse to his heartfelt sentences. If your faith should happen to be at a low point, these luminous pages will restore you."

>—Michael Dennis Browne
>Professor Emeritus, University of Minnesota

Also by William C. Graham:
A Catholic Handbook on Sex: Essentials for the 21st Century, Paulist Press, 2011.
A Catholic Handbook: Essentials for the 21st Century, Paulist Press, 2010.
The Catholic Wedding Book, with Molly Keating, 2nd edition, Paulist Press, 2007.
Clothed in Christ: Toward a Spirituality for Lay Ministry, Twenty-Third Publications, 2007.
Half Finished Heaven: The Social Gospel in American Literature, University Press of America, 1995.

Edited volumes:
Common Good, Uncommon Questions: A Primer in Moral Theology, edited with Timothy Backous, OSB, Liturgical Press, 1996; 2nd edition, Paulist Press, 2014.
Here Comes Everybody: Catholic Studies in American Higher Education, University Press of America, 2008.
Sacred Adventure: Beginning Theological Study, 2nd edition, University Press of America, 2006.
More Urgent Than Usual: The Final Homilies of Mark Hollenhorst, Liturgical Press, 1995.

100 Days Closer to Christ

William C. Graham

LITURGICAL PRESS
Collegeville, Minnesota

www.litpress.org

Cover design by Stefan Killen Design. Illustration: Thinkstock.

Scripture texts, prefaces, introductions, footnotes and cross references used in this work are taken from the *New American Bible, revised edition* © 2010, 1991, 1986, 1970 Confraternity of Christian Doctrine, Inc., Washington, DC All Rights Reserved. No part of this work may be reproduced or transmitted in any form or by any means, electronic or mechanical, including photocopying, recording, or by any information storage and retrieval system, without permission in writing from the copyright owner.

Excerpts from the English translation of *Rite of Baptism for Children* © 1969, International Commission on English in the Liturgy Corporation (ICEL); excerpts from the English translation of Non-Biblical Readings from *The Liturgy of the Hours* © 1973, 1974, 1975, ICEL; excerpts from the English translation of *Rite of Confirmation (Second Edition)* © 1975, ICEL; excerpts from the English translation of *Order of Christian Funerals* © 1985, ICEL; excerpts from the English translation of *The Roman Missal* © 2010, ICEL. All rights reserved.

Excerpts from documents of the Second Vatican Council are from *Vatican Council II: The Basic Sixteen Documents*, by Austin Flannery, OP © 1996 (Costello Publishing Company, Inc.). Used with permission.

© 2014 by Order of Saint Benedict, Collegeville, Minnesota. All rights reserved. No part of this book may be reproduced in any form, by print, microfilm, microfiche, mechanical recording, photocopying, translation, or by any other means, known or yet unknown, for any purpose except brief quotations in reviews, without the previous written permission of Liturgical Press, Saint John's Abbey, PO Box 7500, Collegeville, Minnesota 56321-7500. Printed in the United States of America.

ISBN 978-0-8146-4917-6   ISBN 978-0-8146-3598-8 (ebook)

> What has been, that will be;
> what has been done, that will be done.
> Nothing is new under the sun!
>
> — Ecclesiastes 1:9

> The one who sat on the throne said,
> "Behold, I make all things new."
>
> — Revelation 21:5

> You called, you shouted,
> and you broke through my deafness.
> You flashed, you shone,
> and you dispelled my blindness.
> You breathed your fragrance on me;
> I drew in breath and now I pant for you.
> I have tasted you;
> now I hunger and thirst for more.
> You touched me,
> and I burn for your peace.
>
> — St. Augustine, The Confessions

Contents

Acknowledgments   11

Introduction   13

Ad Astra per Aspera: A Summer's Journey to Restored Faith   17

Advent and Christmas: Sharing the Wisdom of Christ   20

Another Day in Paradise   23

Ash Wednesday   24

Back to School   25

"Behold the Wood of the Cross,
   on Which Hung the Salvation of the World"   27

Beware of False Prophets   29

Bound to Justice; Called to Mercy   31

Brodello   33

Bugia Bearers for the New Age   35

Built Strong by Women   36

Burdens (Lifted) and Grief (Assuaged) in the Paschal Mystery   38

Burial of a Pope   41

Busyness   43

Collaborating in the Church's Work   44

Commandments   46

Commemorating All the Faithful Departed   48

Crèche, Light and Mystery   50

Crock Pots and Holiness   52

Cursed by Interesting Times   54

Divine Mystery Active in Our Lives   55

Eagle Has Landed   58

Enclosing Us for Tender Love   60

Factus Homo Factor   61

Farmers Sowing Seeds   62

Fire Feast   63

Fully Conscious and Active Participation   64

Giant in the Earth   66

Gone Mad with Violence   68

Goodness or Perfection?   69

Grace Is Everywhere   71

Great Things That We Do Not Understand   72

Happy Holidays!   74

Holy Ground on the East Side in the Fourth Pew   76

How Christians Love   78

Illumination, Word, Consummation   79

Initiating the Church's Teaching on Marriage   80

Intensified Identity   81

Is Jesus Anti-Diversity?   82

Is Suffering a Good Thing?   83

Kindness   85

Leisure and the Love of Learning   86

Letter to a Just-Vowed Jesuit   87

Light of Christ, Gently Used   89

Like Winnowed Chaff   91

Love Looks like What?   92

Misery, the Call to Worship, and the Vision of Glory   93

My Evangelical Failure   95

My Evangelical Failure, Part the Second   96

Nones at Christmas   98

Not to Ministering Angels   100

Numbers of the Heavenly Church   101

Our Father   103

Out of the Mouths of Babes   104

Pagan Babies   106

Perfecting Love and Heartfelt Compassion   107

Peter's Chair   108

Phyllis   109

Plumber's Butt: Two Views   110

Polished Arrows, Hidden Quiver:
   Showing in Our Lives the Glory of God   111

Power   114

Profitably Practicing Lent   115

Reconciling Power in the Church   118

Ritual as Teacher   119

Sabbath Sentiments: Awe in the Presence of Majesty   121

Sabbath Sentiments II: Is Sunday (and Are We) in Jeopardy?   123

Sabbath Sentiments III: What Should Sunday Look Like?   125

Sabbath Sentiments IV:
   Sabbath Process Reveals Sabbath Posture   127

Sabbath Sentiments V:
   A Palace in Time; Not a Date but an Atmosphere   129

Saints among Saints   131

Save a Soul by Picking Up a Needle   132

SBNR   133

Sensus Fidelium   135

Serendipitous Wisdom   138

Single or Celibate?   140

Sirens, Whistles, and the Reign of God   142

Some Solstice Thoughts for Winter   144

Speaking of Doors: Shepherd, Gate, and Lamb   145

Stand Tall   147

Summer Peace   148

Sweet Mystery of Life   149

That Mourning Beatitude   150

There Is No Winter in the Church's Year   151

"The One Who Blasphemes against the Holy Spirit Will Not Be Forgiven"   153

Tragedy and the Will of God   154

Transformation in Christ   157

The Tridentine Mass   160

Trying Times   163

Visions of Radiance   165

Washing Feet   166

We Are What We Repeatedly Do   167

What Does Hope Look Like?   168

What Does Justice Look like from Down There, Shorty?   170

What if the Occupy Movement Had Become a Moveable Feast?   171

Who Can Be Saved?   174

Who Is My Neighbor?   176

Window, White Cane, and the Body of Christ   178

Wisdom and Holiness   180

Work of Bees   181

Zed, Z, in Conclusion:
   Running with the "Inexpressible Delight of Love"   182

Acknowledgments

I am grateful to all who, in any way and many ways, have contributed to getting this little book into print.

Some of these essays began life as solitary thoughts and meditations as I have plodded along assorted hiking paths, country roads, and city streets. Some took shape as homilies or classes; many are pieces of articles or reflections published in *National Catholic Reporter*, *America*, *Commonweal*, *Ministry & Liturgy*, *Celebration*, *Homiletic and Pastoral Review*, *Loose-Leaf Lectionary*, and even the *Duluth News Tribune*. They reflect different times, seasons, moods, and methods. In a sense, they capture some of the glory as well as the travail involved in being a person of faith over a number of years, with the assorted opportunities and challenges that such involvement presents. I am grateful to the congregations and classes, the publications and the editors who first helped them see the light of day. I have had great opportunity to road test ideas and thoughts, thus refining and honing as I move along. Father Alfred Deutsch, OSB, of Saint John's Abbey (May he be with God!), told me years ago that the bump and grind of communal living is essential to formation. The years have proven him to be more correct than I was prepared for. Such is life as a child of God, however. It is not a solitary vocation, but one lived in the midst of a church that is not always pacific or peopled in exactly the way that we might have planned. To all who have prompted, shaped, edited, published, appreciated, or criticized these prayerful thoughts, reflections, and provisional essays, I am deeply grateful.

This book began to take shape when I was fortunate to spend a summer week in 2012 at the Collegeville Institute for Ecumenical and Cultural Research as a participant in a writers' workshop, funded by the Lilly Endowment, with the poet Michael Dennis Browne. His good humor and extraordinary skill promoted much good work on the part of all the interesting folks in that group. My submissions to them encouraged me to continue with this collection. I am very grateful to all the folks there, visitors and staff, for so great a gift. To all who assisted, I am happy to offer thanks. These include especially my students at the College of St. Scholastica who patiently read with me and offered wise critiques as the manuscript took shape over a number of semesters. And thanks also to those who listened as I preached and later engaged in earnest dialogue, especially at the parish to which I now belong and of which I was once the pastor, Saint Michael's in Duluth, and also at the Basilica of Saint Mary in Minneapolis, where I am honored to be welcomed among the presiders. At Liturgical Press, Trish Vanni, then the publisher for the parish market, was instrumental in envisioning the possibilities for this little book; and Andy Edwards, the managing editor for the parish market, is a very capable editor to whom I entrust my work without anxiety.

While I am grateful to all who have shaped this little book, its shortcomings are my responsibility alone.

William C. Graham
February 2, 2014
Feast of the Presentation:
> *Treading the path of virtue,*
> *we may reach that light which never fails.*

Introduction

> The goal set before us is no trifling one;
> we are striving for eternal life.
>
> — St. Cyril of Jerusalem, from a
> catechetical instruction.[1]

Each Christian soul experiences precious moments allowing glimpses and feelings of God's mystery. In this, we are as near as most of us will come to a mystical moment: we become breathless with the sudden flash of God's goodness in human tenderness. It is the Word made flesh, God-with-us, who inspires these moments, who lets us see and feel the transformation that sanctifying and actual grace make present. In this wonder of the incarnation we see our God made visible and tangible, and so are caught up in love of the God we cannot see.

The chapters that follow here relate and consider moments of grace, seeing and experiencing the transforming presence of God coming as a gift mediated through an encounter with another person or perhaps a text. Some of these encounters resemble *lectio divina* in that they invite scriptural considerations flowing from the Word or the church's life of prayer that give flashes of insight and meaning on one pilgrim's way. Others may resemble *visio divina* in that they see one thing, consider its beauty or significance, and understand something else. In this way, these encounters are sacramental.

In his lovely little book titled *A Monk's Alphabet: Moments of Stillness in a Turning World*, Benedictine Fr. Jeremy Driscoll notes that his thoughts are offered to provoke the interlocutor, his reader, to join the search. "We proceed in fits and starts," he writes, as no one has the total resolution of the mystery. He notes that Evagrius, a fourth-century monk, would write "centuries," a series of one hundred thoughts. Other writers, in the hundreds of years that have followed, have imitated this form; in it, each thought or meditation stands on its own and works toward its own effect. Driscoll notes, "Life is lovely, life is hard—this is true for me like it is for us all." Monastic life has given him space to think about what we all care about and have to face.[2] He offers a model for thoughtful souls in the twenty-first century as Evagrius did in the fourth. In fact, perhaps he echoes the founder of the first Benedictine monastery in the United States, Boniface Wimmer, OSB, who also brought the Benedictines to Minnesota: "Our motto must be: Forward, always forward"![3]

This book follows in the tradition of Evagrius, though not from a monk's pen or monastery, but rather from a diocesan priest who has been pastor, professor, and writer. One of my brothers-in-law, asked to describe what I do, commented, "He reads books; he thinks; sometimes he writes things down." I am grateful to him for describing it simply; I would add God to the mix. I hope that the Spirit of God somehow directs my reading, thinking, praying, and writing. This forward journey is the path to the unfolding reign of God. Says Jesus, "Repent, for the kingdom of heaven is at hand" (Matt 4:17). Following that path, we discover the benefits of finding wisdom. Mother Scholastica Kerst, OSB, the founder of the Monastery and College of St. Scholastica in Duluth, found her and their motto in the book of Proverbs, which speaks of the benefits of finding Holy Wisdom: "Her ways are pleasant ways, / and all her paths are peace" (3:17).

Any of these one hundred reflections, essays, and provisional thoughts can stand alone to provoke thoughtful prayer. Some may be seasonal; others might be attitudinal. Each seeks to stand before mystery in awe, wonder, praise, and thanksgiving. These four attitudes, awe, wonder, praise, and thanksgiving, I pray, have shaped my life and these reflections. These attitudes do not depend on ecclesial authority; they do not worry about political aspirations; they have no concern with translations or postures. Instead, they seek God where God may be found, in shadow and in light. "Happy the one who finds wisdom, / the one who gains understanding!" (Prov 3:13). And then, once Holy Wisdom, or the road to her, is found: "Sincerely I learned about her, and ungrudgingly do I share— / her riches I do not hide away; / For she is an unfailing treasure; / those who gain this treasure win the friendship of God, / being commended by the gifts that come from her discipline" (Wis 7:13-14). Onward, then, and upward!

Notes

1. Qtd. in *The Liturgy of the Hours*, vol. 3 (New York: Catholic Book Publishing, 1975), 561.

2. Jeremy Driscoll, *A Monk's Alphabet: Moments of Stillness in a Turning World* (Boston: Shambhala, 2006), 3, 4–5, 6.

3. Joel Rippinger, *The Benedictine Order in the United States: An Interpretive History* (Collegeville, MN: Liturgical Press, 1990), 37.

Ad Astra per Aspera:
A Summer's Journey to Restored Faith

I have a former student to whom I am deeply indebted for a lesson in how faith works, suffers, and rebounds. He was a good student, interested in many things in and out of the classroom, good-looking and affable. He spent a fall semester in eager anticipation of his girlfriend joining him at the university; she was to transfer in for the spring semester. She arrived as planned, proved to be drop-dead gorgeous, and as smart and personable as she was beautiful. Together, they took a class from me. Their relationship was admirable. They shared a vision of an impending engagement to be followed shortly by a wedding, and their hopes, aspirations, and dreams were in view as they worked day by day through their junior year in college.

But, as sometimes happens in young love, the relationship went south midway through the semester. There seemed to be no particular cataclysm that precipitated it, no guilty or unfaithful party, just a sad parting. But young Ryan suffered from the symptoms of a broken heart more egregiously than any other disappointed lover in the state of Illinois. He'd sometimes come to my office to mourn, either standing silently in the doorway, head downcast, or sitting listlessly and sighing deeply. I'd tell him from time to time that "The only cure for a broken heart is the passage of time." "Yes," he'd say, "you keep saying so."

But as the semester came to its conclusion, he was not yet healed, or even healing, had failed to register for fall classes, and had lost interest in many of the things that had animated him previously. While he may not have been clinically depressed, he was deeply unhappy, and I was concerned that he might drop out of school or do something else that might be dangerous, foolish, or not in his best interest. He promised, though, to keep in touch. The semester ended and we abandoned the campus.

Ryan lost faith in promises, in young love, in his beloved, in the goodness of human experience. He is, I think, a picture of what the loss of faith looks like. Writing in *America*, Sr. Dianne Bergant, CSA, points out that loss of faith does not have to do with doctrine. We do not wake up one morning doubting the Trinity or questioning the hypostatic union. She suggests that we lose faith in people to whom we had turned, or we judge that life has "taken such a disastrous turn" that not even God can fix it. Living by faith, Bergant suggests, is much more difficult than studying faith. But people of faith "have to live with disappointment and loss and failure, and not give up on other people or on God."[1]

Ryan, in cooperation with God's grace, apparently came to that same insight without having read *America*. On a fine July afternoon, an e-mail message from him popped up on my computer screen: "This summer has actually been good for me. A new perspective on life has opened up for me and I just feel much more relaxed about whatever may come my way. I am very happy with myself, just being the person I want to be. I have met up with old and new friends and am happy with life. Yesterday evening, I was sitting up on my roof just looking at the sky and sunset and colors. It made me happy to be who and where I am. My view was slightly distorted by smokestacks and power lines in the distance, but I looked past those. If something is in my way I find a way around it. So that's how I am. How has your summer been?"

Ryan's note could have been headlined *ad astra per aspera*, "through difficulties to the stars." I am taken with the image of him on the roof at sunset, gazing into the Illinois horizon and beyond. His neighborhood has noxious elements, oil refineries and electric transmission lines. But he can look around, through and beyond these difficulties, delighting in the wonder and promise of God's creation, "the sky and sunset and colors."

He heard the apostle Paul's plan of action and put it to work: he no longer "grieved the Holy Spirit," but put aside bitterness, fury, and anger to live instead a life of kindness, compassion, and forgiveness (Eph 4:30–5:2). Bergant writes that such a choice is faith at work, strengthening us to live in a world filled with disappointment, terror, and violence, and in a church marked by betrayal and disillusionment.

We might reclaim a prayer in loose translation from the Missal of Pius V: "Have mercy on your people, Lord, and give us / a breathing space in the midst of so many troubles."

The enduring faith of the eucharistic communion assures us that we will not lose heart, reforms will not be undone, the church will not wither, and "the one who began a good work in you will continue to complete it until the day of Christ Jesus" (Phil 1:6).

We who walk by faith will not be free from disappointment, but neither will we perish or lose hope. Even in a church scarred and stained, the eucharistic table keeps the light alive and the path navigable. Thanks be to God.

Note

1. Dianne Bergant, "I Doubt It!," The Word, *America* 189, no. 3 (August 4, 2003).

Advent and Christmas: Sharing the Wisdom of Christ

> What the mouth utters, let the mind within acknowledge; what the word says, let the heart ratify.
>
> —St. Ambrose, *On the Mysteries*

"I'm going to study Buddhism. It's so cool!" Jesuit Fr. Richard G. Malloy reports being told by an excited young woman. He responded, "Wow. Did you ever think of studying the religion that teaches that God became what we are so we could become what God is?" Puzzled, she said, "Ooh, that sounds cool. What one's that?" "Catholicism," he answered, the faith in which she had been baptized and confirmed.[1]

How is it that we miss what our prayers make so explicit? Consider the collect (opening prayer) for the Second Sunday of Advent; we ask God that "no earthly undertaking hinder those / who set out in haste to meet your Son, / but may our learning of heavenly wisdom / gain us admittance to his company." There it is: God became what we are so that we can become what God is. How cool is that?

The church's book of prayer is also the church's first catechism; it ought to be our first source when we seek to understand or explain what we believe. For example, the second eucharistic prayer asks God, "Make holy, therefore, these gifts, we pray, / by sending down your Spirit upon them like the dewfall, / so that they may become for us / the Body and † Blood of our Lord Jesus Christ." As the priest prays this, he joins his hands and holds them over the offering. The imposed hands suggest the calling down of the Spirit while the offered prayer states succinctly what we believe happens at the Eucharist.

Both catechists and preachers will be well rewarded by time spent with the Missal in preparing to elucidate our Advent hope and the Christmas mystery. Consider the collect for the Christmas Mass during the day when we pray "that we may share in the divinity of Christ, / who humbled himself to share in our humanity. / Who lives and reigns with you in the unity of the Holy Spirit . . ."

In the solemn blessing that concludes the Christmas celebration, the priest prays, "May the God of infinite goodness, / who by the Incarnation of his Son has driven darkness from the world / and by that glorious Birth has illumined this most holy night (day), / drive far from you the darkness of vice / and illumine your hearts with the light of virtue."

And look at the hope expressed and celebrated later in the same blessing: "God, who by the Incarnation / brought together the earthly and heavenly realm." This wondrous moment climaxes at Easter. In the *Exsultet*, which pictures all creation in exultation around God's throne, even Adam's sin becomes a "happy fault" because it "earned so great, so glorious a Redeemer!" The night of the great vigil of Easter is, then, the "truly blessed night . . . when Christ rose from the underworld!" It is rare to see exclamation points in prayer, but there are five in successive sentences! And here we see the *Exsultet* linked to the Christmas blessing: "O truly blessed night, / when things of heaven are wed to those of earth, / and divine to the human."

In the first weeks of Advent, we look forward not to the birthday of the Christ Child so much as to the second coming of Christ, praying on the first Advent Sunday for "the resolve to run forth to meet your Christ / with righteous deeds at his coming, / so that, gathered at his right hand, / they may be worthy to possess the heavenly Kingdom." This idea is made explicit again in the solemn blessing when the priest prays, "May the almighty and merciful God, / by whose grace you have placed your faith / in the First Coming of his Only Begotten Son / and yearn for his coming again, / sanctify you by the radiance of Christ's Advent / and enrich you with his blessing." And until Christ comes again in power and glory, the blessing asks, "As you run the race of this present life, / may he make you firm in faith, / joyful in hope and active in charity."

On Wednesday of the first week in Advent, we pray again to "[p]repare our hearts, . . . O Lord our God, / by your divine power, / so that at the coming of Christ your Son / we may be found worthy of the banquet of eternal life . . ." This focus on eschatology shifts on the Third Sunday of Advent when we ask God, "who see how your people / faithfully await the feast of the Lord's Nativity, / enable us, we pray, / to attain the joys of so great a salvation / and to celebrate them always / with solemn worship and glad rejoicing." The solemn blessing for the day, however, keeps our eyes fixed on the second coming as it repeats the blessing from the first Sunday (above).

The Fourth Sunday ties Advent to Christmas and Easter as it sums up the paschal mystery in the succinct prayer that those who pray the rosary will recognize: "Pour forth, we beseech you, O Lord, / your grace into our hearts, / that we, to whom the Incarnation of Christ your Son / was made known by the message of an Angel, / may by his Passion and Cross / be brought to the glory of his Resurrection."

The collect for Mass in the morning on December 24 is the last Advent prayer. It unusually addresses Christ himself rather than the Father: "Come quickly, we pray, Lord Jesus, / and do not delay, / that those who trust in your compassion / may find solace and relief in your coming." The prayer takes its inspiration from the penultimate verse of the Bible in the book of Revelation: "Amen! Come, Lord Jesus!" (22:20). "Come, Lord Jesus" is a liturgical refrain from the Aramaic expression *Marana tha* found in 1 Corinthians 16:22. Note that in the embolism, the prayer following the Lord's Prayer before Communion, we ask that God in mercy keep us "free from sin / and safe from all distress, / as we await the blessed hope / and the coming of our Savior, Jesus Christ." Making this prayer, or praying *Marana tha*, is to utter a creedal statement, the church's belief enshrined in the eucharistic Memorial Acclamation: "We proclaim your Death, O Lord, / and profess your Resurrection / until you come again."

Christmas calls us to celebrate the presence of Christ among us. Again and again, our prayers tell us what that means for us. The Preface for the Annunciation, March 25, celebrates the mystery of the incarnation: "For the Virgin Mary heard with faith / that the Christ was to be born . . . for [humankind's] sake / by the overshadowing power of the Holy Spirit. / Lovingly she bore him in her immaculate womb, / that the promises to the children of Israel might come about / and the hope of nations be accomplished beyond all telling." So at Christmas, we pray in the first Preface, "For in the mystery of the Word made flesh / a new light of your glory has shone upon the eyes of our mind, / so that, as we recognize in him God made visible, / we may be caught up through him in love of things invisible."

These orations from *The Roman Missal* continue to be for us a rich source for prayer, reflection, and teaching. We can turn to the apostle Paul for a final, hopeful word: "I am confident of this, that the one who began a good work in you will continue to complete it until the day of Christ Jesus" (Phil 1:6).

Note

1. Richard G. Malloy, "Religious Life in the Age of Facebook: Where have all the young people gone?" *America* 199, no. 1 (July 7, 2008).

Another Day in Paradise

I stopped for gas at my usual place on the way to church recently. In the convenience store there, I greeted the usual clerk, a young fellow in his early twenties. "How's it going?" I asked. "It's another day in paradise," he replied. It didn't seem much like paradise to me with a cold October blast coming in when the door opened by his register, and the odor of yesterday's fried chicken clinging to clothes and skin when the door closed.

It turns out that "Another Day in Paradise" is an award-winning song by Phil Collins, from 1989, written to bring attention to the problem of homelessness. It was a number-one hit worldwide, won the 1991 Grammy Award for Record of the Year, and is ranked number eighty-six on *Billboard*'s Greatest Songs of All Time. The singer invites us to "Think twice."

We people of faith do well to heed the invitation to "Think twice." Paul reminds us that those who have faith are blessed (see Gal 3:7-14). We who have faith are called to live by faith. The psalmist reminds the faithful, "gracious and merciful is the LORD. / He gives food to those who fear him, . . . He showed his powerful deeds to his people" (111:4-6). We who have seen the works and power of God then seek to be among those of whom Jesus speaks: "Whoever is not with me is against me, and whoever does not gather with me scatters" (Luke 11:23; see 11:15-26). Thinking twice, we seek paradise, the reign of God.

Ash Wednesday

Repent, and believe in the Gospel.

— *The Roman Missal*, Ash Wednesday

A college freshmen, called on to explain the concept of mystery, told me, "Mystery is when you are using true words to speak of something that is somehow beyond description and, even with your best efforts, you still don't quite convey much about the topic. It's kind of like talking to a girl about football." Well, one could introduce him to any number of girls and women whose sporting knowledge would cause his theory to crash in flames to the earth. But he does have his finger on something important, doesn't he? The church invites us to enter the mystery of the dying and rising of Jesus. In entering the mystery, we become a new creation.

Lent invites us to enter the mystery of the dying and rising of Jesus. In entering the mystery, we become a new creation. In our annual observance of Lent, we prepare by works of charity and self-sacrifice to renew our baptismal promises, recommitting ourselves to the mystery, reconfiguring ourselves to Christ, seeking to conform ourselves to the Word who moves among us for our salvation. So on Ash Wednesday, as Lent begins, we allow our heads to be signed with ashes because we trust that God is moved by acts of humility and responds with forgiveness to works of penance. The Lenten Preface (III) to the eucharistic prayer explains our Lenten discipline: our self-denial should give God thanks, humble our pride, contribute to the feeding of the poor, and help us imitate God's kindness.

Back to School

I arranged to go on an expedition with one of my nephews one August day in preparation for his entry into first grade. We went off to a Target store and chose first a backpack, then a lunch box, pencils (no pens in first grade!), a large eraser, a notebook, folders, crayons, felt-tipped markers, and then a shirt and pair of slacks. He arranged everything in the cart just so, and transferred everything carefully to the counter when we made our way to the checkout. He politely waited until it was our turn, and then announced good news of great joy to the young cashier: "These are my things! And I am going to be a first grader!"

The cashier appeared to be a high school student, and on a busy summer afternoon might not have cared particularly about her small customer's September destination. But this young woman was uncommonly filled with both grace and wisdom, and she replied enthusiastically, observing that he had all the supplies he needed, seemed very well prepared, and was sure to be successful. He smiled broadly and nodded his agreement and his thanks.

I had just visited a friend before we went to shop, and he had prominently displayed an icon of Peter, having failed to walk on the water, taking the outstretched, helping, and saving hand of Jesus. But here before me in the checkout lane of a suburban Target was a new icon, the same scene, but with new faces. Peter was a small boy stepping out on his excellent adventure, and Jesus was a young woman behind a cash register in a red Target polo shirt. I had not gone to Target expecting to see the face of God, but such surprises are consistent with our tradition. Elijah the prophet looked in all the wrong places, failing to find God in the strong and heavy wind, or in the fire, or in the earthquake, but unexpectedly in a tiny, whispering sound.

I remembered Matthew's account of Jesus about to feed the vast crowd (14:13-21). The disciples wanted to send everyone away to find something for themselves to eat. "You give them something to eat," said Jesus. Here is an important moment in the development of our eucharistic theology: It is not just what God does for us that brings about God's reign; it is also what we do for one another. If my young nephew is always surrounded and supported by family and friends who encourage him, assure him of his possibilities, buoy him up, challenging him and cheering him on, he is sure to be successful in all he attempts, and thus will God's will be done, and the kingdom come. All of our children and, indeed, all of us deserve nothing less.

This grace-filled moment reminds me that in the boat, the church, the wind will die down, we are where we ought to be, and there we will be safe, and there we will meet the Lord. But to get to the boat, to recognize it as the place where we belong, we often need the extended hand that belongs both to Jesus and to each of us. My model today, in fact shipmate of the week, is the young clerk at Target; may she live long and prosper; may all those she encourages flourish; may God's kingdom come, and will be done on earth as it is in heaven.

"Behold the Wood of the Cross, on Which Hung the Salvation of the World"

On Good Friday, we enter with the Lord into Jerusalem to be present with him as he suffers, to stand with Mary as the beloved disciple at the foot of the cross, to weep by the tomb as the stone is rolled in place, and to rejoice with the heavenly powers and all the angelic hosts when Christ, rising in glory, restores our life.

Sometimes on Good Friday, we sing the old spiritual "Were You There When They Crucified My Lord?" This hymn clearly calls to mind the poignant moment in the passion from John's gospel (18:1–19:42; always read on Good Friday) where we hear that Jesus, on the cross, "saw his mother and the disciple there whom he loved." As that disciple is not named, we can claim that spot as our own, singing again, "Were you there when they crucified my Lord?" And "Were you there when they laid him in the tomb?" And "Were you there when God raised him from the tomb?" We claim, each in our own age and place, the identity of the beloved disciple. Each of us can assume the status of beloved disciple. Still, with Isaiah the prophet, we wonder, "Who would believe what we have heard? / To whom has the arm of the Lord been revealed?" (Isa 53:1; see Isa 52:13–53:12).

Further, we trust in the nearness of God, praying as did the psalmist: "Let your face shine upon your servant; / save me in your mercy. . . . / Be strong and take heart, / all who hope in the Lord" (Ps 31:17, 25).

Notice that the solemn celebration of the Lord's paschal mystery, the mystery of the passion and resurrection, begins as we enter Jerusalem with Jesus on Palm Sunday of the Passion of the Lord. And the Sacred Paschal Triduum, the great three days, begins with the evening Mass, Thursday of the Lord's Supper. The Thursday liturgy does not end, though we pause and return to our homes. Note that after the Prayer after Communion, the Blessed Sacrament is carried in procession to the place of repose, and "After a period of adoration in silence, the Priest and ministers genuflect and return to the sacristy" (*Roman Missal*, Holy Thursday, no. 40). There is neither a final blessing nor a dismissal.

On Good Friday, we begin without a greeting. The priest approaches the altar in silence, and prostrates himself while all kneel (no. 5). Then, going to the chair and facing the people, he says a prayer (no. 6). The liturgy that began last night continues now. Later, we will depart in silence (no. 32). Tomorrow, the church waits at the Lord's tomb in prayer and fasting, meditating on the mysteries, awaiting the resurrection (Holy Saturday, no. 1). Our bishops note, "The Easter Triduum begins with the evening Mass of the Lord's Supper on Holy Thursday, reaches its high point in the Easter Vigil, and closes with Evening Prayer on Easter Sunday."[1] This is not just a long but an action-packed, vital, and revitalizing liturgy. We are not simply keeping the memory of what happened once long ago, but have entered with Jesus, as we heard on Palm Sunday, that we might commemorate the entry into Jerusalem, following in his footsteps, made partakers in the cross by his grace, seeking a share in his resurrection and in his life. We are not spectators but rather participants, sharers in the passion and glory of Christ.

We prepare to venerate the cross. Note that we acclaim, "Behold the wood of the Cross, / on which hung the salvation of the world." One of the antiphons that might be sung as we approach explains that we adore the cross, praising and glorifying the resurrection, noting that "because of the wood of a tree / joy has come to the whole world." So we prayed in the solemn intercessions with a vision of paschal joy, asking that God clean the world of all errors, banish disease, drive out hunger, unlock prisons, loosen fetters, granting safety to travelers, return to pilgrims, health to the sick, and salvation to the dying. Such a vision is the gift and grace of God. We who are the beloved disciples honor the death of Jesus today in hope of our own resurrection; we ask that pardon come, comfort be given, holy faith increase, and everlasting salvation be made secure.

Note

1. USCCB Committee on Divine Worship, "Eighteen Questions on the Paschal Triduum," http://old.usccb.org/liturgy/triduumquestions.shtml.

Beware of False Prophets

> Such confidence we have through Christ toward God . . .
> who has indeed qualified us as ministers of a new covenant.
>
> — 2 Corinthians 3:4, 6

As we consider God's offer of covenant and our part in promoting and keeping it, we do well to remember the warning from Jesus in Matthew's gospel: "Beware of false prophets" (7:15). We tend to think, it seems to me, that false prophets are confined to an earlier age, perhaps all done in by Nicaea or Chalcedon or some other council from the distant past. Our temptation is to think that we are living the covenant quite nicely, thank you very much. But perhaps false prophets are with us in every age; they may well be the poor, whom we will always have with us. Our American sense of individualism sometimes leads us, I think, to a false sense of our own importance. Francis Cardinal George of Chicago commented not long ago that many of us who disagree with the church in any number of topics usually assert that the church should change.

Some college students now arrive on campus armed with the phrase "tyranny of relativism." This seems to mean that that whoever or whatever does not agree with them, or with their understanding of what they think they may know or might have been taught of what the church teaches, is simply wrong, relatively speaking, and often heretical, and those who hold those wrong ideas have no rights. We faculty are often even more correct, or think we are, somehow often seeming to believe that we know as much about everything as we knew about our own dissertations on the day of their defense.

We active church members are no exception in this regard. Too often, we think our own take on matters is the only take. Whether we are discussing liturgical translations, the timing of first penance or confirmation, catechetical or bedside approaches, the relationship of ordained to nonordained, the role of women, inclusive language, or any number of other very real issues, we too often deny the church not only infallibility, but even the roles of *mater et magistra*, mother and teacher. When we assume this unfortunate stance of confusing our own perspective with the truth, we take on ourselves the mantle of infallibility in suggesting that the poor huddled masses should profit from our own superior, better understood, and more carefully nuanced view. This is not the humble stance of one who lives under the gospel.

Benedict, in his Rule for monasteries, points to the Psalms: "*God, you have tested us, you have tried us as silver is tried by fire; you have led us into a snare, you have placed afflictions on our backs* (Ps 65[66]:10-11)" (7.40). And Benedict gives us "Tools for Good Works" that will route out the temptation to false prophecy, arrogance, and judgment from our own hearts. We should "live by God's commandments every day" and "shun arrogance." Finally, we should "never lose hope in God's mercy" (4.63, 69, 74).[1]

Note

1. RB quotations are taken from *Rule of Saint Benedict 1980*, ed. Timothy Fry (Collegeville, MN: Liturgical Press, 1981).

Bound to Justice; Called to Mercy

Abraham's bartering with God should not prompt us to do the same. The intent of the inspired story is, no doubt, to convince us of God's mercy rather than to show we can wheedle God down as we ask for things we do not deserve. This important lesson is reflected in the church's long tradition of binding us to justice, but calling us to mercy or charity. Surely God could, in justice, condemn not just the folks of Sodom and Gomorrah for their sins and offenses, but us as well. When we pray the *Confiteor*, remember, we ask God to forgive us for what we have done and what we have failed to do. We often find it difficult to focus on what we have done or neglected to do that might merit punishment or even wrath. It is easier to see the sins of our neighbors, sins either real or imagined, and focus on them rather than to ponder and seek to correct our own failing.

Some folks insist that they know why Sodom and Gomorrah were punished. Their certainty does not have a biblical base. We read simply, in Genesis, that their sin was grave. Note that the folks who interpret the story of Sodom and Gomorrah with certainty nearly always focus on the sins of others, never their own sinfulness. What a cruel and useless position: to see oneself as virtuous, speaking out against the sins of others based on an incomplete or erroneous biblical interpretation. Genesis should make us aware today that each of us comes before God as a sinner. While God could condemn us in justice, he offers mercy to the repentant. Genesis and the church both invite us to focus on our own sin and repentance, our own developing sense of compassion, and the offer of mercy by God to all the waiting world.

In the Lord's Prayer, the only prayer Jesus gave us, we are invited to acknowledge our own inadequacy and dependence. We frail humans ask God to sustain us day by day, holding us up in creation, giving us day by day the bread that we need. Note, too, that we ask to be forgiven. But, and alarmingly, we ask to be forgiven in the way that we have forgiven others. This prayer, usually recited three times daily by early Christians, calls us, then, to lives of mercy and compassion even if we are not good enough to do good for the sake of goodness but only in expectation of a reward: we want to know and experience and be saved by God's mercy and compassion. When we seek to be merciful and compassionate, as Jesus is merciful and compassionate, our hearts will change to be like the heart of Jesus. We who seek this transformation must then attend with newly opened ears to the call of Jesus: "Ask and it will be given to you; seek and you will find; knock and the door will be opened to you. For everyone who asks, receives; and the one who seeks, finds; and to the one who knocks, the door will be opened" (Matt 7:7-8).

Note that the church, in prayer, asks God, the protector of all who hope in him, to bestow in abundance his mercy upon us. We do not ask for that divine mercy because we deserve it. Instead, we look to God as our ruler and guide, and ask that we may use the good things of earth in a way that will assist us to hold fast to those things that endure. And surely mercy and compassion are among the things and the virtues that endure. We ask, too, that God's powerful working of grace in the sacred mysteries sanctify our present way of life and lead us to eternal gladness. The perpetual memorial of the passion of Christ, the gift he gave with love beyond all telling, will profit us for salvation.

Note as well that the church does not single out particular sins or sinners but presumes the sinfulness of us all, and the overwhelming gift of love beyond all telling given to us, unworthy as we all are. This is the attitude of Jesus and his compassionate heart; it is the heart of the prayer and the teaching of the church; it is the call extended to each of us: to live in mercy, in compassion, and in imitation of the saving heart of Jesus.

Brodello

I keep the Christmas cards I receive in a basket, and read them once more before recycling them either on the feast of the Presentation, February 2, or else on Ash Wednesday. There is no religious significance to those dates for the disposal of the previous year's cards; it's just that both days remind me to take care of some clutter both seasonal and domestic. One card that I'll keep this year is from a group of eight college seniors sharing an apartment and their lives as their college experiences come to conclusion. They are pictured standing on the stairs at home, lined up two on a step, posing happily. They look remarkably alike: tall, slender, handsome, and happy. Actually, they look taller than they really are; a couple of them are short. Still, and really, they have lots to be happy about. The most difficult parts of their college careers have been completed; their summer internships went well; their grades are good; their friendships are fruitful; their job prospects are bright. I hope that their dreams come true, and that they remain as happy as they were at the moment the camera flash captured for posterity their youthful vigor and joy.

They are pictured on the Christmas card under the title "Brodello," seeing themselves as a group of bros, brothers. And they really are brothers, a true fraternity, having shared their lives and their hopes, some since early adolescence, and the others since they came to campus as earnest but timid freshmen. And I know they feel terribly clever with the play on words with brodello, their vision of brotherhood, and bordello, a house of ill repute. I appreciate their ironic sensibility, as they are uncommonly virtuous young men.

They are ready now to meet careers and love lives, and to do so with dash and well-earned and deserved confidence. I posted their picture on my office door, and each time I enter, give thanks for goodness, and pray that they will live long and happily in God's grace. Seeing them, as I hope their parents, other professors and teachers, pastors, employers and mentors do, reminds us all that our labors often do bear rich fruit.

I also smile again at the reference to brodello, and delight in how clever they feel about the title. I like to muse that in a decade or two, some eight-year-old will find that card in one of dad's drawers, and ask, "What's a Brodello?" Then she or he will go to Google, and find Urban Dictionary definitions that are far more salacious than the lived experience of said dad and the other bros who really are as upright as the day is long. They have not yet anticipated the day when their young adult humor will come back to greet them in awkward exchanges with children they have hardly yet dreamed about. And we professors, pastors, moms and dads, if we are lucky enough to be alive and present to that moment, can say, as we might promise we will not, "I told you so." But bros they are, and I pray that bros they will remain for the enduring glory of God.

There are others bros—and sisters—who are our neighbors, a cloud of witnesses to human goodness. I have heard that on the occasional evening, some of them in some of our neighborhoods might drink more beer than is prudent, but still: we should see these neighbors as the face of hope, and our great promise for tomorrow.

Bugia Bearers for the New Age

I saw a procession of young women descending the steps after a class yesterday, all in single file, all silently traipsing down while staring intently at their nearly identical iPhones. The phone screens were lighted, the readers were intent; they were as quiet as a procession of nuns filing into chapel in *statio* (according to rank, or date of profession of religious vows) to begin solemn Vespers. And I laughed out loud.

Each bearing a light of a distinctly new kind, they reminded me of the bugia bearers of days long ago. The bugia, palmatoria or scotula, is a low candlestick, with a long handle. It was carried in liturgical processions and before it became an accorded prelate, it was simply to provide light so the presider could pray from the book. In *Jus Pontificalium*, Monsignor Joaquim Nabuco noted in 1956 that the practice of holding a candle by the bishop's side made it easier for him to read in dark churches. Some ancient practices, practical far before they became merely ceremonial, sometimes made very good sense.

Liturgical law decreed that the bugia was a personal prelatical privilege of the bishop, though sometimes its use was granted to canons. I had thought that monsignors could use a bugia too. I may have been incorrect. One rarely sees them these days. Perhaps their use was abrogated in the reform of the liturgy following Vatican II.

The rubrics suggest that the bugia be made of gold or gilt silver for cardinals and patriarchs, but silver for all other prelates. In his book *Costume of Prelates of the Catholic Church*, author Abel Nainfa sniffs, "but this distinction is ever hardly observed in practice." Don't you just hate when that happens!

So, anyway, seeing the procession of young women with lighted phones in a darkened stairwell reminded me of all those bugia bearers bearing bugias. I hope they in that stairwell were and are as attentive to eternal truths as were those earliest prelates who prayed by the light from the bugia-borne candle.

Note

1. John Abel Nainfa, *Costume of Prelates of the Catholic Church* (New York: John Murphy, 1909).

Built Strong by Women

I suggested to the Duluth Benedictines before they elected a new prioress that there have been at least three times when Benedictines might have considered that they had accomplished the mission for which Benedict had initially called them together. Benedict, the father of Western monasticism, seems to have realized that when what some historians call the Dark Ages was about to descend on Europe, learning would not be preserved in all of culture, but would be honored, preserved, and furthered in small enclaves, his monastic communities. Later, as the Renaissance flowered, Benedictines might have thought their work was done. But they remained faithful to their call, continued to seek truth, and enjoyed rejuvenation and redirection at Solesmes and elsewhere. Later yet they came to the new world and built the church here (Duluth's first bishop, James McGolrick, accurately and honestly said in tribute to Mother Scholastica Kerst, "She built my diocese"). The church securely established, once more they could have prayed, with Simeon, "Now, Master, you may let your servant go / in peace . . . " (Luke 2:29).

Because there is a new day dawning with new challenges, I suggested to the Duluth sisters that they stand in the extraordinary gathering space of their Chapel of Our Lady Queen of Peace, put both their hands in the baptismal pool, and consider the mighty female saints who surround them in exquisite stained glass. Looking toward the altar, they see the book of the gospels enshrined on their left and the holy rule on their right. Lifting their eyes beyond the wall in front of them, they might be aware of the field of dreams behind in what they call the Valley of Silence, where they have buried giants in the earth, the women who invited them into monastic communion. These were strong and demanding women who, even in all they suffered, were well aware that fragmentary realizations of the reign of God alone make life worth living.

Lowering their eyes, these sisters see the altar, Christ in our midst, born up by the four angels they have placed at the corners. This table points to and connects with the table set for us in the reign of God before the foundation of the earth. Could one see these sights and, hands wet with baptismal water, proclaim that the work is done and the time is at hand to fold up the tent and disappear into the night? "For the gifts and the call of God are irrevocable" (Rom 11:29).

Religious congregations are largely responsible for building the second largest system (behind only the governmental systems) of educational enterprises, preschools through universities, as well as the second largest health care network in all these United States. And they did it working almost as volunteers, good stewards using their tiny stipends, spending and investing wisely, to build for the reign of God. And they did it all without being accorded social and ecclesial status befitting such accomplishment.

When it is said that the sisters built the church in the new world, this is not just a metaphor but also a literal truth. When I was privileged to be on the faculty of Caldwell College in New Jersey, I would invite students to stand at the classroom window, observing and admiring the Dominican sisters' motherhouse made of red brick with a wide porch and mahogany deck. These bricks had come by train up Bloomfield Avenue and were off-loaded at the foot of the hill across the street from the birthplace of Grover Cleveland. The sisters, in full habit, carried the bricks by hand to their campus at the top of the hill to build their chapel, convent, and high school, with college and health care facility to follow.

Such are the women who built the church in the new world. Thanks be to God.

Burdens (Lifted) and Grief (Assuaged) in the Paschal Mystery

O God,
in whom sinners find mercy and the saints find joy,
we pray to you for our brother/sister N.,
whose body we honor with Christian burial,
that he/she may be delivered from the bonds of death.
Admit him/her to the joyful company of your saints
and raise him/her on the last day
to rejoice in your presence for ever.

We ask this through our Lord Jesus Christ, your Son,
who lives and reigns with you and the Holy Spirit,
one God, for ever and ever.
Amen.

—Funeral Mass, Opening Prayer C,
Order of Christian Funerals

I was called when a young friend went down in a tiny aircraft on the foggy shore of Lake Superior. She was with her two daughters, aged three and four, and her brother-in-law, the pilot. Mom and the pilot died on impact and the children wandered in the woods, burned and frightened, for several hours before their rescue. At her funeral some days later, I would not have wanted to depend on my eloquence or understanding of providence and grace to make sense of this tragedy as the young widower sat in the front pew flanked by her grieving parents and siblings, the four-year-old in a tiny wheelchair, the large congregation stunned and in sorrow.

We did not know why this young wife and mother died, but our ritual and prayer affirmed for us why she lived, and our belief in the communion of saints gave us hope. God's glory was revealed in her: we who were touched in and by her brief life were schooled in the Spirit's gift of awe and wonder; we experienced the transforming power of love; we saw kindness at work and gentleness at play. The incarnate Christ lived in her, and she in Christ. We glimpsed mystery, and God among us. And in the face of this great gift, we blessed the Lord, and gave our thanks.

When the Sacred Congregation for Divine Worship sent forth the Rite of Funerals, revised by decree of the Second Vatican Council and published by the authority of Pope Paul VI in 1969, Benno Cardinal Gut, prefect, and A. Bugnini noted that the church's funeral custom has been "not simply to commend the dead to God but also to raise high the hope of its children and to give witness to its own faith in the future resurrection of the baptized with Christ" (Prot. no. 720/69).

This important piece of Christian practice and teaching sometimes seems lost in modern obituary pages where it is often reported that "at the deceased's request, there will be no services." Anecdotal reports from pastors and funeral directors suggest that this is a mistake on several levels, and that mourning and ritual are important to both individuals and families as well as to the larger community and to the Body of Christ. Even Dominick Dunne's Diary in *Vanity Fair* laments, "I hate it when friends leave strict instructions before they die that there is to be no funeral or memorial service. I've always been a big funeral-goer and a firm believer that surviving friends and relatives need an occasion to be with all the other people who miss the departed the same way they do. You want to hug one another and share stories about the person you all cared about."[1] Dunne seems to agree with St. Augustine, who writes, "All these things—the care of the funeral arrangements, the establishment of the place of burial, the pomp of the ceremonies—are more of a solace for the living than an aid for the dead." The church intercedes for the dead "because of its confident belief that death is not the end nor does it break the bonds forged in life. The Church also ministers to the sorrowing and consoles them in the funeral rites with the comforting word of God and the sacrament of the eucharist" (*Order of Christian Funerals*, General Introduction, 4).

A community gathers around the body of a loved one, making rituals, repeating certain words, singing psalms, hymns, and inspired songs, calling upon God to affirm that love is stronger than death. The Christian community invokes the presence of Jesus risen from the dead, the firstfruits of a new creation that ends not in death but in glory. The message to us is that God invites us to divine life as the perfection of our human journey.

A funeral ritual that fails to affirm this hope is a burden on top of grief, even if it is a fine, feel-good moment in which a human life is remembered and projected into a heaven where dead people now look down on us and smile or play golf with God. The paschal mystery is more than this, and a well-celebrated funeral with powerful preaching invites people to live the mystery now, more generously, ready to risk all because they no longer need fear death.

Good ritual makes all of this clear. The reception and opening of the casket, and the closing of the casket in farewell, the music and prayers, the symbols of light, water, the white pall, the Scripture selections, the homily, the core action of the eucharistic liturgy, Communion, commissioning—all of this conveys powerfully, often to a group of people whose relationship to religion is peripheral, the gospel of Life with all its implications for how the living go forth from church, the cemetery, back into their lives. To be unprepared for or to squander this moment for any reason is to deny people the hope they were promised by the community at baptism.

Notes

1. Dominick Dunne, Dominick Dunne's Diary, *Vanity Fair* (July 2005).

2. Augustine, "The Care To Be Taken for the Dead," in *Treatises on Marriage and Other Subjects*, The Fathers of the Church 15 (Washington, DC: Catholic University of America Press, 1985), 355.

Burial of a Pope

I was awestruck both by the outpouring of emotion and the torrent of information, both news and features, in 2005 as the Catholic world buried Karol Wojtyla, who served the church as Pope John Paul II for 26 years. The reports of millions of people attempting to squeeze themselves into Saint Peter's Square, which holds only 800,000, and our local *Duluth News Tribune*'s own website—where people could "Share your feelings and post your condolences"—testify to the fact that something most unusual was afoot both on earth and in human hearts.

The next generation of scholars, including theologians, sociologists, and historians, will have the task of examining and interpreting the phenomena of these days and years. For Catholic people, as the pope was buried, the immediate task was to be attentive to what the church prays at the time of death, burial, and the nine official days of mourning. An important Catholic principle helps make sense of what the church at prayer is about in the burial of a pope or any other person: *lex orandi, lex credendi*—the law of prayer establishes the law of belief, which is to say that the church's prayer establishes and reveals what the church believes.

The funeral rite for both the pope and any Catholic person begins by evoking the memory of baptism: "In the waters of baptism / [Karol Wojtyla] died with Christ and rose with him to new life. / May he now share with him eternal glory" (Introductory Rites, *Order of Christian Funerals*). The prayer illustrates the sure and certain hope of Christian people that those who have spent their lives in service of God by serving humankind will be forgiven their sins and share in the glory of Christ's resurrection. The first and greatest dignity for any Christian, pope, or person in the back pew comes in being claimed in baptism as a child of God born again in water and the Holy Spirit.

The funeral prayers make it explicit that we do not canonize the dead as saints on the day of their burial: judgment is left to God; and, proclamations of sanctity are left for a later date. It is presumed that all of us have sinned and have fallen short of perfection. We pray for each of those we bury that God will "forgive whatever sins he/she committed through human weakness" (Prayer of Commendation B, *Order of Christian Funerals*). The hymn "Amazing Grace" repeats this theme in reminding us that "grace will lead [us] home."

One of the prayers that begin the funeral of a pope asks God, "grant that your servant Pope [John Paul], / who presided over your Church in charity, / may, with the flock entrusted to his care, / receive from your mercy / the reward of a faithful steward" (Collect C, Prayers for the Dead). The faithful servants include not just popes, bishops, and hierarchy; the faithful are the people of God among whom the pope is numbered. What may be his finest title, servant of the servants of God, expresses this idea of his place among us as one who serves.

An open book of the gospels is usually placed on a bishop's closed casket (remember that the pope is the Bishop of Rome) over his face, to suggest that this Christian lived under the gospel of Christ. The open book also calls to mind the book of the gospels that was held by two deacons tent-like over a man's head when he was ordained a bishop, a reminder and promise to live under the gospel day by day and decision by decision.

Catholic people are usually buried near a church building. The idea is that they have been nourished Sunday by Sunday at the eucharistic table, which points to and connects with the banquet table set in readiness for us in the kingdom of heaven. The pope's funeral was outside, in front of Saint Peter's, to accommodate the enormous crowd but the idea is clearly evident that the Eucharist celebrated in the presence of his body is the foretaste and promise of the heavenly banquet. The Prayer after Communion asks, "As we come to the table of your eternal banquet, / we humbly beg your mercy, Lord, / for the soul of your departed servant Pope [John Paul], / that he may rejoice at last in the possession of the truth / in which he faithfully confirmed your people" (C, Prayers for the Dead).

Perhaps the finest epitaph for John Paul II and any Christian might be found in John's gospel (3:21): "But whoever lives the truth comes to the light, so that his works may be clearly seen as done in God."

Busyness

We who see ourselves in God's service move on in lives of prayer and work. We recognize that the busyness of life causes us to move rapidly from concern to concern, sometimes with friction at our heels. Sometimes we wonder if our prayer life, our *ora*, is as strong as our burdens, our *labora*, demand it be. We remember the dictum of St. Benedict, in the holy Rule for monasteries, that we are to work and pray, so that the prayer of our lips perfects the work of our hands. We make peace with disturbances in our prayer life by recalling St. Vincent de Paul's comforting caution: "Do not become upset or feel guilty because you interrupted your prayer to serve the poor. God is not neglected if you leave him for such service. One of God's works is merely interrupted so that another can be carried out."[1]

Perhaps St. Vincent was reading St. Benedict. Both of them invite us to follow the path of perfection; both of them, too, heard St. Paul clearly as he taught that there are different gifts but the same Spirit, different ministries but the same Lord, different works but the same God who accomplishes all of them in each of us.

We are called to trust the promise of Jesus: God will dwell with us, and the Spirit will instruct us. And so we move on in our lives of prayer and work. Thanks be to God.

Note

1. Vincent de Paul, qtd. in *The Liturgy of the Hours*, vol. 4 (New York: Catholic Book Publishing, 1975), 1425.

Collaborating in the Church's Work

> Give me understanding to keep your law,
> to observe it with all my heart.
>
> — Psalm 119:34

We see a very effective piece of pastoral work and collaborative ministry in the Second Book of Kings. The high priest Hilkiah informs the scribe, "I have found the book of the law in the temple of the Lord" (22:8). The scribe then informs the king to whom the law is read aloud. When the king hears the contents of the book of the law, he tears his garments, reforms his life, summons the elders and all the inhabitants of Jerusalem. He has the entire contents of the book of the covenant read out to them, thus reviving the terms of the covenant. And all the people stand as participants in the covenant. When we consider that story, we tend to pray with the psalmist, "Give me understanding to keep your law, / to observe it with all my heart" (119:34).

Thus formed in our lives and in our ministry, we will continue to pray for discernment. Discernment leads to fullness of life. Irenaeus, remember, tells us that the glory of God is (wo)man fully alive. In the treatise *Against Heresies*, Irenaeus writes, "The glory of God gives life." He also writes that Jesus reveals "to the human race visions of prophecy, the diversity of spiritual gifts, his own ways of ministry, the glorification of the Father, all in due order and harmony, at the appointed time and for our instruction." Not only that, but "where there is order, there is harmony, there is also correct timing; where there is correct timing, there is also advantage." It is for our benefit that God "has made such wonderful arrangements."[1]

Understanding these things intellectually is one thing. To understand them and then to seek to craft our lives in response is to build a spirituality. This is the work of a lifetime. The sooner we begin, the closer we are to the reign of God. As we continue to develop a spirituality for ministry into which we might grow and by which we might continue to be formed, we can be confident that God will raise up prophets in every age. If we cannot be the prophets for this new age and new movement, we will be touched, formed, called, consoled, and challenged by them.

Note

1. Irenaeus of Lyons, *Against Heresies* 4.20.5–7, qtd. in *The Liturgy of the Hours*, vol. 3 (New York: Catholic Book Publishing, 1975), 1498.

Commandments

There is lots of talk in lots of places about the Ten Commandments and where they should be enshrined: on civic property, or someplace else. I propose that placing monuments inscribed with the commandments someplace else might, in the end, safeguard religion and protect our religious freedom.

The commandments are clearly religious in nature. They define not simply a social order or code of law, but our relationship to the creator. The first commandments define our relationship to God, calling us to acknowledge one God, the creator. We are to honor the holy name and imitate God's creative genius, observing the Sabbath, pausing as God did on the seventh day, stopping labor, enjoying and admiring all of creation. (Christians, since the resurrection, have transferred that observance to Sunday, the first day, sometimes referred to as the eighth day, when the risen Christ makes all things new.)

The remaining commandments define our human relationships, and are often seen as the basis of all civil law. This understanding prompts some to seek public display of the commandments. This may not be good religious reasoning.

It is unlikely that when Moses came down from Mount Sinai bearing the tablets of the commandments that the folks awaiting him below found any of the laws novel in any way. No one could have said, "Look, Martha, we can't murder anymore! It is against the law now!" These commandments that define social order are much the same in any society that seeks civility and the common good. What was new when Moses descended with his holy burden was that now these laws defined not just human relationships, but God's covenant within human activity. Our relationship to God is reflected in the way we attend to these laws. God commands us to keep these laws if we wish ever to see him face-to-face.

Asked which of the commandments was the greatest, Jesus replied, "You shall love the Lord, your God, with all your heart, with all your soul, and with all your mind. This is the greatest and the first commandment. The second is like it: You shall love your neighbor as yourself. The whole law and the prophets depend on these two commandments" (Matt 22:37-40). If one loves God, then she or he will love neighbor as a consequence of the first love of God.

So, we Christians are to show our faith in our works and in our relationships. The Letter of James makes that point: "I will demonstrate my faith to you from my works" (2:18). (Luther considered this letter "an epistle of straw," but it remains in the Scriptures nonetheless.) When we Christians are dismissed from worship on Sunday, we may be told, "Go in peace, glorifying the Lord by your life." Our departure is not simply going home, but a commissioning: we are sent to bring the peace we have celebrated into the marketplace and our neighborhoods. We go to be agents and disciples of peace.

The commandments are not for us religious people first and foremost a code of civil law. They are the measure of how we keep covenant with God. One can keep the social commandments (1) to stay out of prison, (2) because it is a good thing to do and promotes one's own welfare and the common good, or (3) to give evidence that one honors God and seeks to do the divine will while keeping the covenant made with our ancestors and made new in Jesus the Christ.

We can keep the law for any of the reasons listed above. Religious people keep the law for the last reason, which we see as the most noble.

So, as our courts have ruled, these commandments are clearly religious in nature. Perhaps they do not belong in courtrooms or on other public property in a society where not all citizens share the same religious perspective. God himself tells us where these commandments ought to be enshrined: "I will put my laws in their minds / and I will write them upon their hearts. / I will be their God, / and they shall be my people" (Heb 8:10).

Commemorating All the Faithful Departed

All Souls' Day is called the Commemoration of All the Faithful Departed in the Roman Missal. We pray that day, in the opening Collect (1), that our faith in the resurrected Christ be deepened, so that our hope of resurrection for those who have gone before us in death also find new strength. The Prayer over the Offerings asks that God's departed servants be taken into glory with Christ in whose great mystery of love we are united. Finally, the Prayer after Communion asks that they pass over to a dwelling place of light and peace. As we make these three prayers, the prayers themselves tell us why we pray for the dead, and how we should pray for them. Once again, we can observe that the church's prayer book is the church's first catechism; what we pray is what we believe. What better way to teach our children and instruct ourselves than to read, ponder, and pray over the texts we use when the church gathers to pray.

For example, every Christian consideration of death must include and be rooted in the hope of the resurrection. And the mystery of the resurrection includes the dying and rising of Christ, and our own participation in that mystery beginning in the waters of baptism. The third eucharistic prayer, when used in Masses for the Dead, speaks of the one who has died as united with Christ in a death like his; we pray that the deceased may also be one with Christ in his resurrection.

This hope of the resurrection inspires artists and poets as well. Samuel Medley's 1775 hymn "I Know That My Redeemer Lives" is known to most of us. Singing it, we get the clear idea that the author was moved by both Job's discovery of the nearness and majesty of God and the later joy of the resurrection. Job fuels our own desire when he asserts his faith: "from my flesh I will see God: . . . my own eyes, not another's, will behold him: / my inmost being is consumed with longing" (19:26-27). The hymn prompts us to sing of our faith in the resurrection: "I know that my Redeemer lives; / What comfort this sweet sentence gives! / He lives, He lives, who once was dead; / He lives, my ever-living Head." The hymn concludes with a vision especially appropriate for us today: "He lives and grants me daily breath; / He lives, and I shall conquer death: / He lives my mansion to prepare; / He lives to bring me safely there."

We know with faith-filled certainty that Christ lives to bring us where he is; we have heard Jesus speak prayerfully to the Father in John's gospel: "I wish that where I am they also may be with me, that they may see my glory that you gave me." The Spirit continues to move among us and live in our hearts, sanctifying us, seeking to bring to fulfillment the continuing prayer of Jesus, as he asks the Father, "that the love with which you loved me may be in them and I in them" (17:24, 26; see 6:37-40).

We will want to sing with gusto the hymn to which these Scriptures gave birth: "He lives, all glory to His name! / He lives, my Jesus, still the same. / Oh, the sweet joy this sentence gives, / 'know that my Redeemer lives!'" The prayer (or embolism) that concludes our recitation of the Lord's Prayer before Communion tells us how we wait for the Lord: We ask God to grant peace in our days, that by divine mercy, we be both free of sin and safe from distress or anxiety as we await Christ. For his are the kingdom, the power, and the glory now and forever.

Crèche, Light and Mystery

> All of us, gazing with unveiled face on the glory of the Lord, are being transformed into the same image from glory to glory, as from the Lord who is the Spirit.
>
> — 2 Corinthians 3:18

Our best Christmas memories are filled with sweetness, with divinity swaddled in Mary and Joseph's love, with human tenderness enfolding the babe, announcing and celebrating the mystery of God among us. Light, joy, peace, and lowing animals are all part of the picture and the memories.

The plaster of paris nativity scene at my local parish prompts memories and anchors gladness. The three kings have often been featured coming slowly from the church's eastern radiators, moving closer day by day, until their arrival at the crèche on the feast of the Epiphany. The set was repainted by volunteers in a ceramics class in the 1980s when I was pastor there at St. Michael's in Duluth; the $38 we gave them for paint and supplies was one of the smallest but best-spent checks I ever signed. We had and they have the same set at St. Rose Parish in Proctor, Minnesota, where I grew up; there are many just like it across the nation. The simple scene can be misleading, though. Mary and Joseph radiate holiness and serenity; they seem untouched by fear, hunger, or chill. Jesus seems not to be fazed by having been delivered in an animal shed and laid in their feeding trough; the scene is not as antiseptic as the birthing places where most of us landed.

The animals in the scene make no rude or smelly noises; they never drop loads that would mess up your shoes or carpets. Karen Sue Smith observes that the Christmas card image of the Savior's birth "does not describe adequately the world into which Jesus was born. God entered a dark, broken world, rife with squalor, violence and suffering, a world that needs a savior. What generates Christmas light and joy is God's presence in that world."[1]

The mystery is Christ among us.

Note

1. Karen Sue Smith, "Two Surprise Guests," Faith in Focus, *America* 197, no. 21 (December 24, 2007): 26.

Crock Pots and Holiness

At the center of Christian life is the setting of the table, the making of Eucharist. We should always be aware that every table points to the eucharistic table where we receive the foretaste and promise of the paschal feast of heaven. With this understanding, we hear St. Benedict in his Rule for monasteries insisting, "regard all utensils and goods . . . as sacred vessels of the altar" (31.10). Apparently crock pots are holy. And we meet Christ at every table, so the Christian person should have a relaxed and hopeful presence whenever folks come to the table. This gathering and being gathered is the task and goal of life and ministry. We should be the expert and the example.

We should be the people who can set the dining room table and gather around members of the Body that is Christ. We will be both richer and more capable when we know how to chat and dine after our own labors have produced the feast. Some insist that they are too busy or do not know how to cook. Nonsense. First, we are as busy as we choose to be. Second, it takes no talent at all to be busy. Third, being a workaholic is not a virtue. Fourth, we all eat.

And cooking is not that difficult. Try this: Buy a crock pot; do not spend much. Buy a beef roast, any cut, about half a pound per person. The less expensive cut it is, the better it will taste after slow cooking. Buy also potatoes, one per person, and carrots. And a bottle of red wine or six-pack of beer. And a bag of salad. Wash the potatoes, but do not peel them, and cut them into chunks. Put them at the bottom of the crock pot. Peel and cut up the carrots, or use those that are precut. Toss them in. Put the roast on top of the vegetables. Pour a cup of wine or sweet vermouth or a can of beer over the roast. Season it. If judging how to season it seems too daunting, buy an envelope of onion soup mix and rub it into the meat. This all can be prepared the night before and refrigerated till morning, but do not add the liquid until you're ready to begin cooking. Plug in the crock pot, turn it to low, and leave it alone for eight to twelve hours. Serve. With the salad.

And whatever wine or beer remains. Folks will praise you. There is an important series of lessons to be learned in this disproportionate response to a small effort.

We all know many lonely people, some because of circumstances that will pass, some because they are awkward in relationships. Here is an opportunity to gather not just our friends and fans, but those who might be especially grateful not just for the food, but more especially, the good company. Scholars point out that the Last Supper in Luke's gospel is the culmination and completion of the table ministry of Jesus seen at least seven other times throughout the gospel.[1] We should keep this in mind. Reflecting on the Last Supper will call us to remember our eucharistic theology and reconsider our own dining practices as we approach our tables. Our eucharistic celebrations and our own festive meals must be both inclusive and reconciling. The second Eucharistic Prayer gives us a vision of what is accomplished both at the altar and at the dining room table: "Humbly we pray / that, partaking of the Body and Blood of Christ, / we may be gathered into one by the Holy Spirit." Not all bread need be consecrated, but it should all be blessed.

Note

1. Edward Foley, "Which Jesus Table? Reflections on Eucharistic Starting Points," *Worship* 82, no. 1 (January 1, 2008): 52.

Cursed by Interesting Times

We buried one of my high school teachers not so long ago, and at the wake I chatted briefly with a woman who had been a friend of his. She asked what I was doing these days and, told that I teach theology, she asked sharply, "Do you teach that God is a man?" "No," I said, "I teach *Catholic* theology." I saw an equally unhappy friend of hers more recently when, some months ago, I presided at a reunion Mass for a Catholic institution. This friend, also long absent from the eucharistic table, sat glumly through the service. Both of these women, intelligent and articulate, suffer from love-hate relationships with the church of their youth, which they have largely abandoned in their disappointment.

There is, frankly, much to disappoint them in our decidedly imperfect communion. One hesitates to invoke Bill Clinton's "I feel your pain," but how to respond to those who so suffer is a problem. We live in a church scarred and stained by sin. Our leaders have disappointed us and, many charge, have squandered the church's authority in dealing with the issues surrounding the sexual abuse crisis. While wanting in justice to compensate victims, local churches then suffer the loss of programs and employees, services and real estate as millions of dollars are paid in reparation to scores of victims. One wonders who is driving the bus, the bishops or their lawyers. If resolution is beyond their immediate episcopal control, some critics charge that the bishops then turn their authority to what can be controlled: the norms for the celebration of the liturgy. Issues such as who can fill the eucharistic cups when, or at which moment extraordinary ministers can enter the sanctuary, some charge, become problems of division and control more than helpful norms for a reverent celebration of Christ among us. Others, including the two women mentioned above, charge that the church is beyond sexist in dealing with women.

If the church is as imperfect as it seems, why not move on? Is there a schism about to happen? Or are all these things simply evidence that we live under the curse of interesting times in a developing church? Or do we pray with Peter as our model, "Master, to whom shall we go? You have the words of eternal life" (John 6:68).

Divine Mystery Active in Our Lives

We buried a federal judge not so long ago, a mighty pillar of the local church and an exemplar as a servant of the law. As we sang the judge to his grave, as we brought his body up the hill for burial in sure hope of resurrection, we struggled with the mystery of life and death, with the threat and the promise of our own mortality. Consoling his family, we consoled ourselves by remembering this man of great integrity, celebrating his many virtues that enhanced life for his family, for us, and for our community. But if we are truly to remember him, if we really mourn his passing, if we hope to meet again, we must cherish those whom he loved, recount those things he taught us, revere the institutions he revered, and imitate the love that quickened him, thus ensuring his continued memory in our midst. All of this became clear in the unfolding liturgy, the public reading of the transforming Word, and the celebration of the Eucharist.

The ritual well done is itself a kind of structure for the human process of grief, enabling the bereaved to accept the fact of death but then guiding them to hope. The homily is a chance to explicate this progress toward faith, but the ritual itself possesses a genius for accomplishing the actual catechesis. A good presider goes with the ritual's flow. And the ritual (*Order of Christian Funerals*) makes clear what its General Introduction stresses: "The community's principal involvement in the ministry of consolation is expressed in its active participation in the celebration of the funeral rites, particularly the vigil for the deceased, the funeral liturgy, and the rite of committal" (11). An initial pastoral visit to a family after a loved one's death "can be important as the first tangible expression of the community's support for the mourners." Additionally, "A minister unfamiliar with the family or the deceased person can learn a great deal on this occasion about the needs of the family and about the life of the deceased" (Prayers after Death, 103). The church's ministries are exhorted to "involve the family in planning the funeral rites" (General Introduction, 17) and to encourage family members "to take an active part" in the ministries at the various celebrations, though "they should not be asked to assume any role that their grief or sense of loss may make too burdensome" (ibid., 15).

Throughout all the rites leading to the grave, Scripture provides both comfort and direction: "The readings proclaim to the assembly the paschal mystery, teach remembrance of the dead, convey the hope of being gathered together again in God's kingdom, and encourage the witness of Christian life." And, above all, they "tell of God's designs for a world in which suffering and death will relinquish their hold on all whom God has called his own" (ibid., 22).

The ritual also clearly states, "A brief homily based on the readings is always given after the gospel reading at the funeral liturgy and may also be given after the readings at the vigil service; but there is never to be a eulogy." The homilist is to be "attentive to the grief of those present," dwelling on God's compassionate love and on the paschal mystery. Rather than eulogize, "The homilist should also help the members of the assembly to understand that the mystery of God's love and the mystery of Jesus' victorious death and resurrection were present in the life and death of the deceased and that these mysteries are active in their own lives as well." The homily thus provides both "consolation and strength to face the death" with "hope nourished by the saving word of God" (ibid., 27). Priests often point out that priests themselves often violate this charge when burying their brother priests.

We often see the gospel writ large in the lives of the faithful we bury and do well to make those homiletic references. But canonization must be left for a later date. We gather to pray that God forgive whatever sins the deceased may have committed; we do not announce her or his arrival in heaven. To do so is inappropriate on many levels, usurping God's authority and presuming a knowledge known to God alone. A quick canonization is dangerous business because it overlooks the human flaws that all of us have. Plaster of paris saints do not have such flaws. If we rush to sainthood and into plaster those who have gone before us, the real danger is that we will not call ourselves to measure up to them, excusing ourselves from duty because saints are saints and we are but flesh and blood.

But this immediate canonization is less likely to happen if the family has other opportunities—perhaps as part of the vigil—to tell stories, laugh, cry. For most families, this needs to happen somewhere, and most understand that this important and personal expression of memory, grief, and hope really should not infiltrate the liturgy that is larger than the individual being buried. The vigil is an opportunity for the gathered family and friends to rejoice in their memories: "At the vigil the Christian community keeps watch with the family in prayer to the God of mercy and finds strength in Christ's presence" (Vigil for the Deceased, 56). The judge mentioned above was well and lovingly remembered by a procession of family, friends, colleagues, and neighbors. This gathering went on as long as those present needed to continue. Those with other obligations, or who tired out more quickly, were free to leave at a time they chose. This approach honors those who wish to speak but leaves the funeral Mass unencumbered with eulogies and remembrances. Part of the genius of the Roman Rite is that it is spare, and in that simplicity, truth and beauty are reflected and celebrated.

Eagle Has Landed

One fine July day, I was sitting in front of my little house on a small lake in northern Minnesota in the late afternoon. A bald eagle landed with a tremendous splash in the lake; his wingspan was close to six feet, and he made his way clumsily up the bank and onto the dock. This eagle has lived on a small peninsula in the lake for a couple years, but I had never before been so close to him or to any eagle. Clearly, something was unusual here. After ten minutes on the dock, he walked up the bank, rested another twenty or thirty minutes, and tried to fly away. He could not lift off but narrowly missed broadsiding the neighbor's boathouse. He rested again, and finally flew away, returning about an hour later to perch in a lakeside tree, and then left, I hope, for home.

We take our eagles very seriously in northern Minnesota. I called the DNR shortly after the first landing; they wanted to know if I was sure it was an eagle. Well, it was not a duck or a loon; he was gone, however, before they could send someone out. But unusual occurrences call us to be mindful of circumstances and events. The bird may have lead poisoning; perhaps there is something else going on in the lake we have not yet noticed. His distress calls us to vigilance.

Not just nature, but business, too, calls us to pay attention even when we think all is well. Consider what we might learn from the Swiss. In his book *Rethinking the Church*, James Emery White offers an interesting piece of business history: For over two centuries, the Swiss made the best watches in the world, constantly refining their expertise. They invented the minute hand and the second hand; they pioneered better manufacturing of gears and mainsprings. They led the way in waterproofing techniques and self-winding models. By 1968, the Swiss made 65 percent of all watches sold in the world, claiming profits of up to 90 percent. But between 1979 and 1981, fifty thousand of the sixty-two thousand Swiss watchmakers lost their jobs. They controlled less than 10 percent of the world market and their profit domination dropped to less than 20 percent. According to White, the Swiss had refused to consider the Quartz movement since it had neither mainspring nor knob. Such a change was unimaginable for them. But not for Seiko and others who took over leadership in the watch industry. What we might learn from the Swiss watchmakers is both profound and, well, timely. A history that was profitable, secure, and seemed dominant was destroyed by an unwillingness to consider the future or to rethink a business approach.

It might be wise for us who live under the Gospel to consider lessons both from nature and the business world as we keep one eye on the past and another on our future. We must be open to transformational possibilities so that we can be transformed. What does this renewed life look like? The Polish poet Juliusz Slowacki has some sense of that when he writes, in "My Testament," that after death an "unseen force" crushes, transforming "bread-eaters into angels."[1] He calls to mind Ignatius of Antioch who, early in the second century, was arrested, condemned to death, and transported to Rome to die in the arena. In anticipation of his martyrdom, Ignatius wrote, "I am God's wheat, ground fine by the lion's teeth to be made purest bread for Christ."[2]

We bread-eaters are called to become more perfectly that which we already are: the Body of Christ. We ought, then, to pay careful attention to situations and circumstances: for sometimes a visit from an eagle is not just a social call. Sometimes a change in technology is not one that can simply be ignored in hopes that it will go away in favor of business as usual. And most times a free lunch is not just about food.

Notes

1. Juliusz Slowacki, "My Testament," trans. Walter Whipple, http://www.mission.net/poland/warsaw/literature/poems/testamen.htm.

2. Ignatius of Antioch, Letter to the Romans, qtd. in *The Liturgy of the Hours*, vol. 4 (New York: Catholic Book Publishing, 1975), 1490.

Enclosing Us for Tender Love

Paul reminds us of the dignity that is ours by virtue of our baptism: "through the Spirit, by faith, we await the hope of righteousness." He asserts that what counts is "faith working through love" (Gal 5:5-6). Faith works through love when we are brought up from the baptismal water, and clothed in a white garment. The priest or deacon says to the new Christian, "You have become a new creation, and have clothed yourself in Christ. See in this white garment the outward sign of your Christian dignity. With your family and friends to help you by word and example, bring that dignity unstained into the everlasting life of heaven" (Explanatory Rites 99, Rite of Baptism for Children).

Julian of Norwich, writing in the fourteenth or fifteenth century, reflected that "Christ is our clothing, who for love / Wraps us up, holds us close, entirely / Enclosing us for tender love."[1]

At a Catholic funeral, when the body is welcomed at the church door (much as the candidate for baptism was welcomed at the church door on the day of her or his baptism), the priest blesses the body with holy water, a reminder of baptism. A white pall is placed over the casket to recall the baptismal garment. By these actions at the beginning and end of our lives, and every day in between, we seek to conform ourselves to Christ who tells us, "give alms, and behold, everything will be clean for you" (Luke 11:41).

Note

1. Julian of Norwich, *Showings*, trans. Edmund Colledge and James Walsh, The Classics of Western Spirituality (New York: Paulist Press, 1978), 183.

Factus Homo Factor

I visited the venerable Benedictine monastery of Christ in the Desert in the mountainous wilderness above Santa Fe, New Mexico, and read this on the wall in the guest dining room in Latin and English: *Factus homo factor hominis factique redemptor iudico corporeus corpora corda deus* (Having been made man, I, the Maker of Man, and Redeemer what I have made, judge, having myself a body, the bodies and souls of men: for I am God).

This saying is copied from a mosaic in the cathedral, begun in 1131, at Cefalu, a small coastal town in Italy about fifty miles east of Palermo. The mosaic in the church's apse depicts Christ *Pantocrator* in the church's apse. The *Pantocrator* is the Ruler and Sustainer of the world. One of the ways that we are sustained is that the earth, ruled by Christ, provides grain and grapes for all our needs. As a man, Jesus understands our needs. As God, he provides for them. He redeems what he has made: us. But those bodies he has redeemed he also judges, for he himself has a body. But he is God.

What a wondrous reflection to post in a dining room where guests eat in silence. How more wondrous yet for the rest of us to post it in our hearts, that we might always remember the compassionate generosity of the Creator. And we remember, too, that he judges our use of the gifts. No wonder the saints invite us to moderation in all things (except moderation itself, I guess).

Farmers Sowing Seeds

Here is what we know about Wisdom from the biblical book of the same name: "she is the reflection of eternal light, / the spotless mirror of the power of God, / the image of his goodness. / Although she is one, she can do all things, / and she renews everything while herself perduring; / Passing into holy souls from age to age, / she produces friends of God and prophets" (7:26-27). We who wish to be numbered among those friends of God must go deliberately about it, always and all ways and everywhere.

One of my former colleagues modeled that posture for me one day, the first of a semester some years ago. We closed our office doors, greeted each other silently, and walked together in the direction of our classrooms. As we took our first steps, she said quietly and with a satisfied smile, "The farmer goes out to sow the seed" (see Luke 8:5). I heard that as both an observation and a prayer, for the sowing of seeds is a faithful, hope-filled act. What is planted seems to die, but later yields a harvest. The sowing of seeds is not just a faithful, hope-filled act; it is also the beginning of wisdom.

Parents and teachers inspire the young not so much with facts or information, but with ideas and dreams when they model both a love of learning and the desire for God. These seeds, sown on the rich soil of the human spirit, "bear fruit thirty and sixty and a hundredfold" (Mark 4:20).

Fire Feast

February 2 is a fire feast, another of the days on which we employ flame to speak of the One Light. The feast of the Presentation of the Lord occurs forty days after the birth of Jesus. It is also known as Candlemas Day, since the blessing and procession of candles is included in the day's liturgy. The prayer over the candles that will be used in the year's liturgies are blessed by the priest who invokes God, the source and origin of all light, "who on this day showed to the just man Simeon / the Light for revelation to the Gentiles." We humbly ask God that, "in answer to your people's prayers, / you may be pleased to sanctify with your blessing + these candles, / which we are eager to carry in praise of your name, / so that, treading the path of virtue, / we may reach that light which never fails."

The baptismal liturgy invites us to keep the flame of faith alive in our hearts so that when the Lord comes, we may go out to meet him with all the saints in the heavenly kingdom. That ritual moment is remembered on the feast of the Presentation as the blessed candles are carried by the processing people into church. The priest invites them, who are gathered by the Holy Spirit, to "proceed to the house of God to encounter Christ. / There we shall find him / and recognize him in the breaking of the bread, / until he comes again, revealed in glory."

Simeon, the just man, once saw the Light; so also can we!

Fully Conscious and Active Participation

The liturgy, like the Church,
is intended to be hierarchical and polyphonic,
respecting the different roles assigned by Christ
and allowing all the different voices to blend
in one great hymn of praise.

> — John Paul II, address to the bishops of
> the Episcopal conference of the United
> States (1998)

There we were in our Way of the Pilgrim class pouring over the text of *Egeria's Travels*, the fragmentary account from the fourth century of a nun's journey to the Holy Land from what is now Spain. I paused, looked at one of the young scholars, and asked, "Nick, can you ever remember having had this much fun ever before in your life?" He met my gaze confidently. "No," he answered. "I cannot remember a single other instant in which I have had this much fun." Well, I appreciated his enthusiasm even if his veracity was not entirely above suspicion. Nick was engaged in an ancient, important text, and looking for clues about the nature of pilgrimage. With his seminar mates, he radiated a happy sense of satisfied purpose.

Nick's beatitude, I think, was reflective of those who came to Jesus in chapter 6 of Mark's gospel. We read that people recognized Jesus. "They scurried about the surrounding country and began to bring in the sick on mats to wherever they heard he was. Whatever villages or towns or countryside he entered, they laid the sick in the marketplaces and begged him that they might touch only the tassel on his cloak; and as many as touched it were healed" (vv. 55-56). We who seek Jesus will feel the power flowing from his touch and from our attempts to touch him. This is our Christian quest. Liturgy is our vehicle.

Remember Simon telling Jesus, "Everyone is looking for you" (Mark 1:37). This is the company to which we are called, to be part of the great crowd looking for Jesus. Pope St. Leo the Great, who reigned from 440 to 461, observed that whatever was visible in Christ has passed over into the sacraments. And here is what was visible in Christ: inclusion for the isolated, health restored to the sick, light for those in darkness, food for the hungry, drink for the thirsty, balm for the afflicted, healing for the sick, sight for the blind, and new life for the dead. This inclusionary sense is what prompted the fathers of the Second Vatican Council to teach:

> It is very much the wish of the church that all the faithful should be led to take that full, conscious, and active part in liturgical celebrations which is demanded by the very nature of the liturgy, and to which the Christian people, "a chosen race, a royal priesthood, a holy nation, a redeemed people" (1 Pet 2:9, 4-5) have a right and to which they are bound by reason of their Baptism.
>
> In the restoration and development of the sacred liturgy the full and active participation by all the people is the paramount concern, for it is the primary, indeed the indispensable source from which the faithful are to derive the true Christian spirit. Therefore, in all their apostolic activity, pastors of souls should energetically set about achieving it through the requisite formation. (*Sacrosanctum Concilium* 14)

The vision of those who have participated in the quest is described in the first Eucharistic Prayer for Reconciliation: "Help us to work together / for the coming of your Kingdom, / until the hour when we stand before you, / Saints among the Saints in the halls of heaven."

Giant in the Earth

Consider the story of Mother Alfred Moes, the foundress of the Joliet (Illinois) Franciscans in the late 1800s, a group dedicated to education and health care. At some point before Joliet was a diocese and when their territory was still part of the Archdiocese of Chicago, the archbishop, annoyed for some reason with Mother Alfred, came to the motherhouse, which shared a campus with what has become their University of St. Francis. The archbishop overstepped his authority and demanded that the sisters not reelect Mother Alfred—and they acceded to his unreasonable request. Here is a woman who could have exploded with righteous anger. Instead, she apparently intuited what Augustine is alleged to have said, that Hope has two lovely daughters, Anger and Courage. Mother Alfred left Joliet with those two virtuous daughters and, together with a small band of sisters, started north.

When she got to Rochester, Minnesota, she met there some young doctors, brothers, who told her that the place needed a good hospital or clinic and while they were capable doctors, they did not quite know how to set up such an enterprise. "Okay, boys," she said, "you be the doctors and I'll take care of the rest." And thus was born the world-famous Mayo Clinic in the estimable shadow of the Rochester Franciscans on Assisi Heights. This story was first told to me by a recently deceased Joliet Franciscan; whenever I have heard the tale, the archbishop has no name (reminiscent of the rich man in the Lazarus story in Luke 16). Mother Alfred, however, will live in glory, "carried away by angels to Abraham's bosom" (Luke 16:22).

The sisters remember that her inspiration was Psalm 37: "Commit your way to the Lord; / trust in him and he will act / And make your righteousness shine like the dawn, / your justice like noonday." Sister Maria Pesavento, a later president of the Joliet Franciscans, writes that "Mother Alfred's pioneering zeal does inspire us and we continue to listen to the Spirit and trust that God will act through each of us."

What are the challenges ahead? How can we think that they could be less painful or less glorious than those endured and enjoyed by our ancestors in the faith? God will give us grace to endure, to seek transformation in grace. And grace will lead us on: flares of special grace will light our way. And there are among us even now new giants in the earth, filled with God's good Spirit, who will lead us to freedom.

Paul reminds us that "where the Spirit of the Lord is, there is freedom. All of us, gazing with unveiled face on the glory of the Lord, are being transformed into the same image from glory to glory, as from the Lord who is the Spirit" (2 Cor 3:17-18).

And, having "this ministry through the mercy shown us, we are not discouraged" (4:1), "For the gifts and the call of God are irrevocable" (Rom 11:29).

Gone Mad with Violence

Amadou Diallo, a twenty-two-year-old immigrant from Guinea, was shot and killed in New York City on February 4, 1999, by four New York City Police Department plain-clothed officers. He had worked, selling goods from a folding table, just blocks down the same street in Manhattan on which I lived. Unarmed, he was fired at with forty-one bullets. Commenting sadly, the late John Cardinal O'Connor, then the archbishop of New York, said, "We have gone mad with violence."

On December 14, 2012, a twenty-year-old man slaughtered twenty-six children and adults at a Connecticut elementary school, having first shot and killed his mother in her home, and then himself after his rampage.

Telling the tale of the slaughter of the Holy Innocents, Matthew writes, "Then was fulfilled what had been said through Jeremiah the prophet: 'A voice was heard in Ramah, / sobbing and loud lamentation; / Rachel weeping for her children, / and she would not be consoled, / since they were no more'" (2:17-18).

Rachel's weeping is heard in every age. Though we may have gone mad with violence, we hear John, calling us "Beloved," telling us, "Now this is the message that we have heard from him [Jesus] and proclaim to you: God is light, and in him there is no darkness at all." Further, "if we walk in the light as he is in the light, then we have fellowship with one another, and the blood of his Son Jesus cleanses us from all sin" (1 John 1:5, 7).

On the feast of the Holy Innocents, December 28, we remember that they confessed and proclaimed God's glory, not by speaking but by dying. We ask in prayer that the faith we confess with our lips may also speak through the way we live. This is our only hope in a world gone mad with violence.

Goodness or Perfection?

John Paul II addresses the issue of attending to moral teaching in a lively and direct way in his masterful consideration of the dialogue of Jesus with the rich young man in his encyclical *Veritatis Splendor* (1993). John Paul notes that Matthew does not name the young man who comes to Jesus inquiring, "what good must I do to have eternal life?" (Matt 19:16-21), so in him, "we can recognize every person who, consciously or not, *approaches Christ the Redeemer of man and questions him about morality.*" He points out that the question before the young man "is not so much about rules to be followed, but *about the full meaning of life.*" In the seeking, God, our origin and goal, can be heard beckoning to us (6, 7).

Those who "wish to go to the heart of the Gospel's moral teaching and grasp its profound and unchanging content" must inquire carefully into the meaning of the rich young man's question and, "even more, the meaning of Jesus' reply, allowing ourselves to be guided by him. Jesus, as a patient and sensitive teacher, answers the young man by taking him, as it were, by the hand, and leading him step by step to the full truth" (8). He notes, "*To ask about the good,* in fact, *ultimately means to turn towards God,* the fullness of goodness" (9). Further, "*What man is and what he must do becomes clear as soon as God reveals himself.*" Thus, "*The moral life presents itself as the response* due to the many gratuitous initiatives taken by God out of love for man" (10).

John Paul notes that "it is clear that Jesus does not intend to list each and every one of the commandments required in order to 'enter into life,'" but instead draws the young man's attention to "the summary (cf. *Rom* 13:8-10) and foundation of which is *the commandment of love of neighbour:* 'You shall love your neighbour as yourself' (*Mt* 19:19; cf. *Mk* 12:31)," in which is found "a precise expression of *the singular dignity of the human person*" (13). The young man seeks more. "The Good Teacher invites him to enter upon the path of perfection: 'If you wish to be perfect, go, sell your possessions and give the money to the poor, and you will have treasure in heaven; then come, follow me' (*Mt* 19:21)" (16).

Jesus calls the young man to a life of perfect love, though it is clear that he is already both good and beloved and on the path to the fullness of God's reign. So what do we seek, goodness or perfection?

Grace Is Everywhere

Annie Dillard, in her "mystical excursion into the natural world," quotes a story of Martin Buber's: "Rabbi Mandel once boasted to his teacher Rabbi Elimelekh that evenings he saw the angel who rolls away the darkness before light. 'Yes,' said Rabbi Elimelekh, 'in my youth I saw that too. Later on you don't see these things anymore.'" Dillard observes that "beauty and grace are performed whether or not we will or sense them. The least we can do is try to be there."[1] The apostle Paul reports that "grace was given to each of us according to the measure of Christ's gift" (Eph 4:7).

George Bernanos's wonderful novel first published in 1937, *The Diary of a Country Priest*, also alerts us to the fact that "Grace is everywhere." We who seek transformation in Christ do well to be aware of the presence of grace. This is God's gift "for building up the body of Christ, until we all attain to the unity of faith." So, "living the truth in love, we should grow in every way into him who is the head, Christ" (Eph 4:12-13, 15). And so we pray that we, like the good tree, "may bear fruit in the future" (Luke 13:9).

Note

1. Annie Dillard, *Pilgrim at Tinker Creek* (New York: Bantam Books, 1974), cover, 31–32, 8.

Great Things That We Do Not Understand

> What is man that you are mindful of him,
> and a son of man that you care for him?
> Yet you have made him little less than a god,
> crowned him with glory and honor.
>
> — Psalm 8:5-6

Seeking the fullness of God's reign, but only almost there, we call on God as children in the night. Annie Dillard observes that Christian worshipers "come at God with an unwarranted air of professionalism, with authority and pomp, as though they knew what they were doing." We "saunter through the liturgy like Mohawks along a strand of scaffolding who have long since forgotten their danger. If God were to blast such a service to bits, the congregation would be, I believe, genuinely shocked."[1]

But dangerous grace will lead us on: flares of special grace will light our way. We look for leadership on the issues that threaten the unity of our church. We understand that all issues in the life of the church cannot be resolved easily or quickly. We understand that transformation in Christ will include openness to new situations and new needs. We look for leaders to be pastoral and sensitive but also bold and visionary in speaking to the issues of our time while identifying and maintaining what is essential to our tradition. We look for leadership also in our attempts to name God, seeking new ways and additional images to reflect divinity, grace, love, and communion as we move toward consensus with all the church's ecumenical partners.

In the coming among us of the Word made flesh, the ineffable God became both visible and tangible. Today, however, seeking to see the face of Christ seems to have become more complicated. So if we call on God as the Source of All Being, or as Creator, Redeemer, and Sanctifier, we are not wrong. We do not mean to reduce God to function or render God impersonal. But because there is nothing uniquely Christian in those terms of address, they may tell us less about the triune God than about us and how our search for the Way is complicated by lack of clarity about human relationships. We cannot lose sight of the prize: intimacy with God through our friendship with Jesus on which everything depends.

If we are angry about what we perceive to be patriarchy or misogyny, and if we bring that anger to prayer, we might do well to remember the counsel of Rabbi Abraham Heschel: "In a controversy, the instant we feel anger, we have already ceased striving for truth and have begun striving for ourselves." The rabbi's daughter Susannah points to her father's interpretation of the Sabbath rest: "Ye shall kindle no fire—not even the fire of righteous indignation." She also remembers his comment, "It is a sin to be sad on the Sabbath."[2] In this light, we Christians are at great risk when we bring anger and indignation to the baptismal font or eucharistic table.

We continue to wonder about the significance of the maleness of Jesus, and are perhaps as confused and conflicted in our own age as ever has been the case in the church's whole history. As we consider issues of gender and human sexuality, we do not have a clear vision of justice or equality. Kilian McDonnell, OSB, helps us frame life's complications in his poem "Joseph, I'm Pregnant by the Holy Ghost." He writes as Mary might have spoken: "Life was simple before that angel / pushed open the kitchen door, / announced light and trouble, as though / a foe had roiled the bottom of the well / and now the pail brings up only / murky water." In "God Cheats," he writes of Jacob's experience in Genesis 32:25, which we share: "I wrestle with a stranger until dawn breaks, / sweat to sweat, flesh to mystery."[3]

As we move on, seeking God, stumbling to name divinity in our midst, we do well to remember how "Job answered the LORD and said: . . . I have spoken but did not understand; things too marvelous for me, which I did not know" (42:1, 3). But we live in a Spirit-filled age that inspires and inflames our hope, awaiting the fulfillment of the promise of Jesus that "the Spirit of truth" will "guide [us] to all truth." This Spirit "will declare to [us] the things that are coming" (John 16:13).

Notes

1. Annie Dillard, *Holy the Firm* (New York: HarperCollins, 1977), 60.

2. Doris Donnelly, "Lovingly Observant," An interview with Susannah Heschel, *America* 196, no. 21 (June 18, 2007).

3. Kilian McDonnell, OSB, *Yahweh's Other Shoe* (Collegeville, MN: Saint John's University Press, 2006), 18, 8.

Happy Holidays!

[M]ay we come to share in the divinity of Christ
who humbled himself to share in our humanity.

— The Liturgy of the Eucharist

A few years ago on an Advent Sunday in one of our parishes up north, a very sincere woman took my hand in both of hers as she left Mass, and said gravely, "Happy Holidays." I wondered which holidays she had in mind. Perhaps the Solstice? Maybe Super Bowl Sunday?

My little rant here is not against diversity, inclusivity, or sharing. I appreciate that all peoples and every culture wants, even needs, to celebrate a midwinter festival. Winter in northern Minnesota is hard, dark, and long. When the earth turns and the days begin imperceptibly to grow longer, not everyone sees theological insight, christological promise, and liturgical metaphor. Some wish simply to celebrate the light and its promise of spring and summer when we can return to the beach. For some people, that is clearly either good enough or all they want. And I want to extend a wish to that particular group of self-proclaimed freethinkers: "Happy Holidays!"

We Christians assert that we have our eyes and our hearts fixed on something better and more poetic. For us Christians, these Advent days are about watching and waiting. We do not wait for the birth of the baby Jesus. Those who are attentive to the news know that happened long ago. In Advent, we wait for the second coming: that same Jesus who was born in a stable, wrapped in swaddling clothes, and laid in a manger grew in age and in wisdom and will come again in glory as the Just Judge. And so we wait in joyful hope. Our intent is that when he comes, he will find us watching in prayer, engaged in good works, our hearts filled with wonder and praise.

In the collect for the Second Sunday of Advent, we ask the God of power and mercy that "no earthly undertaking hinder those / who set out in haste to meet your Son, / but may our learning of heavenly wisdom / gain us admittance to his company."

In our Advent of watching and waiting, and in our Christmas joy, we celebrate the true light that conquers darkness, the one who lights our paths, who causes the flame of faith to burn in our hearts. We know that the Word became flesh and dwelt among us. Jesus, the Word of God, humbled himself to share in our humanity. He promises that we will come to share in his divinity. This is the true holiday; it is the holiest of days.

So here is the reason Christians celebrate at Christmas: our good cheer, our festivity, and our giving of gifts are all in imitation of the first giver of gifts, the God of creation who preempted Hallmark cards in being the very first to send the very best—Jesus the Christ in whom we see the light and find the way.

We might pay attention to G. K. Chesterton, who commented on humanity's slow drifting away from God; when that happens, he wrote, we find nothing but "cures that don't cure, blessings that don't bless and solutions that don't solve"[1] Advent gives us a chance to take up the prophet's task and remind each other that there is more to life than our immediate wants.

The Scriptures that the church appoints for the Advent season move us to be alert, to be aware and wary. The apostle Paul says it is time to wake from sleep. Matthew's gospel warns us to stay awake and not be caught unaware. "Be prepared," Jesus warns. The call is to the peaceable kingdom that Isaiah the prophet envisioned when swords would be beaten into plowshares and spears into pruning hooks. Paul tells Christians how to prepare for the second coming of Christ: throw off works of darkness and put on the armor of light.

Advent is our opportunity to rekindle in our own souls and hearts the power of God's presence and, in turn, to make that truth apparent to others by thoughtful prayer and active concern. The joy we anticipate should be balanced by a true sense of preparation, getting our hearts and homes ready for the coming of the Lord as we wait in joyful hope.

Note

1. Qtd. in Martin Luther King, Jr., "The Man Who Was a Fool," *Strength to Love* (Minneapolis: Fortress Press, 1981), 75; original source unknown.

Holy Ground on the East Side in the Fourth Pew

God's grace and God's presence are forever around us, even when we are oblivious to the transformation to which they call us. Stephen Martin observes that "we forget about grace as we sweep floors and sit in traffic and stagger around a dark room in the middle of the night hunting for lost pacifiers; then we remember, and then we forget again."[1] The gift of Christmas allows us to see grace, to name it, to claim it, and to let it shape our lives. When we see grace at work, we need to shout it out. Sometimes, at least for me, it takes years for the process of giving and receiving to be unveiled for us as the great grace that truly is at work.

One of my first Sundays as pastor at St. Michael's back in the day, I stood before the presider's chair for the Sunday Eucharist and saw in one of the first pews the young son of two parents I had known since high school; the child, then about four or five, stared intently at me. Even when we sat for the first reading, he did not move his eyes, but settled into the pew. As the reader approached the lectern, I looked back at the boy, met his stare, and winked at him. Then, I turned quickly to focus on the lector and the Scripture. But I kept an eye on the boy; his eyes opened wide in surprise; he elbowed his father and whispered to him what had happened. The father was patient; he nodded in understanding, and patted the boy lovingly. After Mass, after the crowd had left, father and son were waiting. "You'll never believe what this one told me," the amused but disbelieving dad said. He related the story of the wink. I looked down at the little guy, but said nothing. His eyes were wide in amazement. Or something.

The boy grew to be a man, faithful Sunday by Sunday at the eucharistic table with his family; we never discussed the Sunday wink. Eventually, he went away to college and later began a successful career in a neighboring state. I went away first to New York and then to Chicago, usually returning there for Mass at midnight on Christmas. One year not so long ago, the young man was back in town for Christmas and with all the family sat in the very same pew where so many years of Sundays they had worshiped together. The service began and, just as he had once done so many years before, the young man stared intently at me. When he was sure that I was returning his gaze, he cocked his head just a bit, and winked at me. And I laughed out loud.

His father looked at me, looked at his son, and winced at both of us laughing in church. After Mass, waiting once again as he had years earlier, he took us each by an elbow, pulled us close, and said, "Okay, you two, you've got some explaining to do." And so we did.

Really, I felt that I, in imitation of Moses, should have taken off my shoes, for I was standing on holy ground. The kid's wink and laugh and sharp memory were a sacrament of God's good presence, of the transforming activity of Christ. The young man's good humor highlighted the holy ties that bind us together at this table and in that season.

Note

1. Stephen Martin, "Brother Lawrence and the Chimney Bird," Faith in Focus, *America* 197, no. 21 (Dec. 24, 2007): 28.

How Christians Love

A recent book by a Cistercian monk from Australia, Michael Casey, offers insight that is remarkably helpful for us who seek God either inside or outside of a monastic enclosure. In the book, *The Road to Eternal Life: Reflections on the Prologue of Benedict's Rule*, he notes that "compromises to our integrity will cause us to experience an uncomfortable degree of disappointment and frustration at our lack of progress." The "subtle voice of conscience singing" invites us back. However, "Discipleship is more than wistful thinking."[1]

Jesus starts us on the road that goes beyond wishful thinking to real conversion and true discipleship. His way is not about an initial enthusiasm that soon burns out when the difficulties of life assert themselves. He encourages us on the journey, and, in fact, simplifies things a great deal for us when he says, "Be merciful, just as your Father is merciful. Stop judging and you will not be judged. Stop condemning and you will not be condemned. Forgive and you will be forgiven" (Luke 6:36-37). When we can do as the Teacher asks and models, then all God's people will readily observe how Christians love one another.

Note

1. Michael Casey, *The Road to Eternal Life: Reflections on the Prologue of Benedict's Rule* (Collegeville, MN: Liturgical Press, 2011), 61.

Illumination, Word, Consummation

Looking at the spaces for ritual activity in a Catholic church, one will better understand both who we Christians are and what we hope to become:

The baptistery is the place of illumination; here we are enlightened by and in Christ, buried with him in the waters of the font, then rising with him to newness and fullness of life.

At the ambo, we are reminded of the angel atop the empty tomb proclaiming the message of the resurrection. Here we hear the word of God and are challenged to conform ourselves to it.

The altar is the place where we bring our gifts of bread and wine, "fruit of the earth and work of human hands." Infused with the Spirit of God, they become for us the Body and Blood of Christ, at whose command we celebrate the mysteries. We consume what we have offered and the Spirit has transformed, but we too are transformed into what we have consumed. Our charge, according to St. Augustine, is to become more perfectly that which we already are: the Body of Christ. We do not just consume, but are consumed into the very mystery of Christ among us. Consummation suggests the completion not of the task of assembling, hearing, offering, praying, eating, and drinking, but a fulfillment of what we are with a vision of what we hope to become. This consummation is a divinization: we pray that we may become that which we have received.

Initiating the Church's Teaching on Marriage

We should be clear today that when the apostle Paul wrote to the Ephesians, he was not seeking to describe how marriage should work in every age, place, and instance, for surely that was not his intent. Paul wrote in eager and joyful anticipation of the second coming of Christ; his writings make it clear that he thought Christ would come soon, certainly in his lifetime. This did not leave him time to consider the future of either slavery or marriage.

Instead, he is instructing us in what he terms "a great mystery." He explains, "I speak in reference to Christ and the church" (Eph 5:32). Here is the beginning of the church's teaching on the sacrament of marriage. He instructs, "Husbands, love your wives, even as Christ loved the church" (5:25; see 5:21-33). This is spelled out for us in the collect (B) for the celebration of marriage, which asserts that in the wedding covenant, God foreshadows the sacrament of Christ and his church. The love of husband and wife is sacramental in that we see in it the very love of God. In the nuptial blessing, we hear that the love of the spouses foreshadows the covenant God made with us. The mystical marriage of Christ with the church is to be manifest among the faithful in the union of husband and wife. So we ask, "What is the kingdom of God like?" (Luke 13:18). The beginning of the answer is made especially apparent in married love. Married people, both blessed and burdened, must attend to Paul's instruction: "each one of you should love his wife as himself, and the wife should respect her husband" (Eph 5:33).

Intensified Identity

Paul tells us, "In him [Christ] we were also chosen" (Eph 1:11). This idea is supported by our ritualized activity in making our way to church and getting ourselves assembled around the altar. Liturgical theologians point out that the entrance procession concludes when the ministers reach the altar, but it begins far earlier and involves all of us. Each of us moves in response to God's call, leaving our homes and coming to the place where we are known by the titles church or people of God. We are individuals or families as we leave home, but by the door of this building, the procession intensifies and we are identifiable as a congregation. The entrance of the priest completes the procession and we become a sacramental showing forth of the church in a particular place and throughout the world.

Our actions around book and table reveal the truth about our common identity. The many of us who have been gathered have become a single body. We do not make ourselves this people, but we have been called and gathered by God to be his very own. We are to understand then that we are not saved as individuals, but as a communion of believers. Our gathering at this table anticipates the heavenly banquet.[1] We come in response to the call of God and thus realize that the church makes the Eucharist, and the Eucharist makes the church.

Note

1. See "Theology of the Latin Text and Rite," by Dominic Serra in *A Commentary on the Order of Mass of* the Roman Missal (Collegeville, MN: Liturgical Press, 2011), 125–26.

Is Jesus Anti-Diversity?

Sometimes and in some places, the message of Jesus causes division between those who seek to follow the Gospel call and those who reject it. The concern of Jesus is not to be heard or understood as anti-diversity. While we believe and profess that all salvation comes through Christ, we seek to understand and appreciate the value and dignity of other traditions and religions. Pope John Paul II noted in his book *Crossing the Threshold of Hope*[1] that God can work outside the church and outside the sacraments. No one is outside God's saving power. The church routinely prays to God for all who seek God with sincere hearts (see the fourth eucharistic prayer). Speaking of other religious traditions, the Second Vatican Council (1962–65) taught, "The Catholic Church rejects nothing of what is true and holy in these religions. It has a high regard for the manner of life and conduct, the precepts and doctrines which, although differing in many ways from its own teaching, nevertheless often reflect a ray of that truth which enlightens all men and women" (*Nostra Aetate* 2).

So we make Paul's prayer our own: "Now to him who is able to accomplish far more than all we ask or imagine, by the power at work within us, to him be glory in the church and in Christ Jesus to all generations, forever and ever. Amen" (Eph 3:20-21).

Note

1. John Paul II, *Crossing the Threshold of Hope*, ed. Vittorio Messori (New York: Knopf, 1994).

Is Suffering a Good Thing?

What Paul writes to the Colossians can be disastrously misunderstood: "Now I rejoice in my sufferings for your sake, and in my flesh I am filling up what is lacking in the afflictions of Christ" (Col 1:24).

First, is suffering a good thing? Should we seek out opportunities to suffer? And how is it that our suffering fills what is lacking in the afflictions of Christ? Next, Jesus the Christ is the incarnate Word, the very visible and tangible Word of God. What could be lacking in the one who is God from God, light from light, true God from true God, through whom all things were made?

We should note that Paul does not solve the problem that provoked Job and millions (or billions!) of people before and since: why does the just one suffer? There is no available answer to that question, as God, speaking from the whirlwind, made known to Job. The just and the unjust will suffer. It is part of our human condition, the consequence of our humanity, of original sin. Paul does not attempt to solve the unsolvable, but gives us a Christian context for enduring what we must. He tells his brothers and sisters, "Now I rejoice in my sufferings for your sake." He is suffering, but endures his suffering for the sisters and brothers, for the Body of Christ. Because the church exists among people on earth, and because suffering is part of the human condition, because there will be suffering in every time and place, Paul endured his suffering and we, too, must endure our sufferings as members of Christ's Body. We endure what we must in hope, as Paul writes, "to bring to completion for you the word of God, the mystery hidden from ages and from generations past" (Col 1:25-26). So the sufferings of Christ are incomplete because we, members of the Body of Christ, still suffer; with this understanding, we can join Paul in asserting, "Now I rejoice in my sufferings for your sake, and in my flesh I am filling up what is lacking in the afflictions of Christ."

In this way, we live not as fatalists or pessimists, but as God's hopeful people, knowing that suffering will not rob us of our human dignity, but our sufferings are joined to those of Christ and his Body, the church. While we do not seek out suffering, we do know that we have the opportunity to face suffering in such a way as to enhance rather than diminish our human dignity.

We look in the Scriptures for models of the just, and of those noble in their sufferings. We remember Abraham and Sarah who had lived long and justly but had no children who might care for them in their old age. Visited by divine messengers, Abraham hears, "I will return to you about this time next year, and Sarah will then have a son" (Gen 18:10). While they may have thought their lives were about to end, they were invited to embark on an extraordinary journey foundational to the birth of Jesus and the salvation of all the world. Even in our suffering, we share in the glory of Christ. For this great gift, let us bless the Lord, and give God thanks.

Kindness

Plato, the Greek philosopher, born in 427 BC, the teacher of Aristotle, is often quoted in a reminder appropriate for every person in every age and place: "Be kind, for everyone you meet is fighting a harder battle."

The Talmud, Judaism's holiest book that explains and builds upon the Torah, instructs, "Deeds of kindness are equal in weight to all the commandments" (TJ Pe'ah 1:1).

John Wesley, one of the founders of Methodism, is said to have taught, "Do all the good you can, by all the means you can, in all the ways you can, in all the places you can, at all the times you can, to all the people you can, as long as ever you can."

Dietrich Bonhoeffer observed, "We must learn to regard people less in the light of what they do or omit to do, and more in the light of what they suffer."[1] As a German Lutheran pastor and theologian involved in the German resistance movement against Nazism, he was executed in April 1945, shortly before the end of the war. It's staggering to consider he could think as he thought even as he suffered as he did, isn't it?

We should all talk that talk and walk that walk. Then, we can write the next aphorism to inspire those who will follow. Your first draft can begin here:

_____
_____
_____
_____
_____
_____.

Note

1. Dietrich Bonhoeffer, "Contempt for Humanity?," in *Letters and Papers from Prison*, ed. Eberhard Bethge (New York: Macmillan, 1971), 10.

Leisure and the Love of Learning

Leisure is essential if one is to be a proper university student or professor. Only in leisure are ideas born and connections made and learning both enjoyed and accomplished. One of the delights of this kind of essential leisure is the daily rubbing of elbows, the bump and grind of life together. At lunch, a liberal arts professor may inquire of a colleague from the sciences how it is that in the Mexican dish chicken mole the chocolate somehow subdues the fiery peppers. At coffee, an English professor might inquire of a Bible scholar if the confusing use of pronouns in most English translations of the gospels reflects pronoun confusion in the original, ancient texts, or if the problem is a modern or English one. These interlocutors model interdisciplinary inquiry. It is not a new phenomenon but is as old as the academy, as old as scholarship, as old as conversation and learning.

Beginning students sometimes see learning as happening in compartments: an English box, a math container, a science unit, a fine arts compartment, a theology space. Once the compartments have been filled, the requirements met, a degree is granted. One who sees education in this filling station approach may remind a theology professor who demands that students write in complete sentences with subjects and verbs that "This is not an English class," as if English is only studied to be used in an English class, and not so that one may more effectively communicate any number of ideas and questions in any discipline. This student has yet to read the Letter to the Romans (8:28): "We know that all things work for good for those who love God, who are called according to his purpose."

An interdisciplinary approach looks everywhere, to literature and literary interpretation, to theology, to history, to popular culture, always seeking to understand what seems to be a new phenomenon but that, in reality, is not all that innovative. Perhaps it is in this way that seekers will encounter the face of God.

Letter to a Just-Vowed Jesuit

August 11, the Feast of Saint Clare,
whose prayer before the Blessed Sacrament
   for the protection of her sisters
invited and provoked the divine response:
"I will keep them always in my care."

Dear Paul,
    This morning, youthful, vigorous, and radiantly happy, you moved up confidently and joyfully to kneel on the altar steps. Watching you ascend called to mind the song of the psalmist: "Let them bring me to your holy mountain, / to the place of your dwelling, / That I may come to the altar of God, / to God, my joy, my delight" (Ps 43:3b-4a). Or, as some remember it translated, "I will go to the altar of God, to God who gives joy to my youth" (Ps 42:4, Vulgate). You knelt as the presiding provincial superiors held before you the consecrated bread and wine, the Body and Blood of Christ. Then, in the presence of your superiors and confreres, your family and friends, and all the assembled church, you pronounced your vows. With your companions, you promised to enter the Society of Jesus "to spend my life in it forever." You acknowledged that God had freely given you "the desire to make this offer" of your total commitment, and asked that he give you as well "the abundant grace to fulfill it." And the church said, "Amen!"
    The preacher had reminded you, and all the congregation, of how deeply the founder, St. Ignatius of Loyola, prized imagination, and how all of you had been sent, in your novitiate adventures, to direct involvement with and life among the poor, the isolated, the alienated, and the dispossessed. What a wonderful confluence of delight and duty: to be imaginative always in the service of the people and reign of God.
    You have found companions for your great journey, a fine company of gentlemen. Seeing you begin the vowed journey in that company of your fellows was greatly moving. Religious life allows and invites a

certain quirkiness: ponytails, clergy collars with running shoes; smiles so filled with joyful hope that even teeth shine; academic dreams and disciplines of every possible variety; fond embraces and quiet satisfaction; plans and prospects, and missioning to travel and study, awe and wonder. All of this, and all of you, are some of the best moments of hope that our church could possibly see in this new century.

One of your university classmates, now living out promises of a different sort, told me recently in a phone conversation that he was blowing dust off his computer keyboard while at his not very interesting job, wondering what life would have been like if he had elected a riskier but more adventuresome path. You will, I pray, never make such a phone call or feel such a void. Rather, may you always recognize and rejoice in the many opportunities and resources afforded you in the great company of Jesuits. Saint Bernard insists, "It is not enough to live entirely for Christ. One must have done it for a long time." May you be granted both graces.

In your years of study ahead, you will no doubt distinguish yourself as both scholar and seeker. I am grateful to have walked some initial steps with you, and look forward to the fulfillment of your great promise. With St. Paul, "I am confident of this, that the one who began a good work in you will continue to complete it until the day of Christ Jesus" (Phil 1:6).

Your fan,
Bill G.

Light of Christ, Gently Used

Working one Wednesday as a volunteer at my parish's Used-a-Bit Shop downtown in Duluth, I found for sale on a table near the front door a baptismal candle used just a bit and still in its cardboard presentation box. I have given many, hundreds, of these candles out to parents and godparents who moved solemnly to the paschal candle, lighting the new candle for the newly baptized from the Light, which is Christ. After the candle has been lighted, I have spoken as the church directs:

> Parents and godparents, this light is entrusted to you to be kept burning brightly. These children of yours have been enlightened by Christ. They are to walk always as children of the light. May they keep the flame of faith alive in their hearts. When the Lord comes, may they go out to meet him with all the saints in the heavenly kingdom. (Explanatory Rites 64, Rite of Baptism for Children)

Emerging from the baptismal waters, we have experienced directly and intimately the Source of all life and holiness. The candle's glow signifies our sharing in that radiance, an external sign of what has been ignited internally. Attentive to the mystery's ritual, we see that baptism is the source for all rights, responsibilities, and charisms for Christian people. Reflecting on and renewing our baptismal promises ought to move us to consider promises not kept and goals unattained; looking at the baptismal candle ought to invite us to sing again the words of the Easter Vigil's *Exsultet*, first sung in the glow of the paschal candle as we ask God to "accept this candle, a solemn offering, / . . . the praises of this pillar, / which glowing fire ignites for God's honor / . . . Therefore, O Lord, / we pray you that this candle, / . . . may persevere undimmed, / to overcome the darkness of this night."

We light bearers seek to come to maturity as Christians, fully engaged with Christ in the redemption of all the world. Aware of this dignity and responsibility in all and each of the baptized, a friend told me early in the Easter season, "I wrote a journal entry when my son was baptized almost twenty-one years ago, reminding myself then and him in the future that this was the most important moment in his life. I need to dig it out, reconsider the truth of it as he prepares to head from his Jesuit university to a fall semester in El Salvador, the land of martyrs. Baptism allows grace to perfect nature, and if this happens within a conscious community of the baptized, the results can be quite remarkable—the whole revealed as more than the sum of its parts." The youthful pilgrim goes off alive with light while his father repeats and claims a prayer from the *Exsultet*'s final stanza: "May this flame be found still burning / by the Morning Star: / the one Morning Star who never sets."

But I had not thought much of what might happen to the candle after its ritual presentation. Sometimes I have advised a nervous godfather to extinguish the candle before returning it to the box from which it had been slipped before the ceremony. I occasionally remember having read pious advice from a new mother that the baptismal candle should be lighted annually on the baptismal anniversary. And that bride and groom should bring their candles to church on their wedding day, jointly to kindle the wedding candle from the two baptismal candles.

The little baptismal candle carries a lot of freight, symbolism, and memory for something that costs just a dollar or two and is made from paraffin rather than beeswax. And all of that, or at least the paraffin, could be had at the Used-a-Bit for just a dime. What happened to the child who received that light? Why is that candle, apparently burned for just a minute or two, not burning annually or being carried to a wedding's unity candle?

Does the one who was baptized remember being enfolded in "God's holy people, set free from sin by baptism" (blessing of the water, 54), and becoming "a new creation . . . clothed . . . in Christ" (clothing with a baptismal garment, 63), as well as one of the "children of the light" (presentation of a lighted candle, 64)?

In the gospel, Jesus tells us that the kingdom of heaven will be like ten maidens who went out to meet the bridegroom. Five of them were foolish. They brought no flasks of oil. Their lamps burned out. They missed the banquet.

Let it not be so for the candle-less child. "For God who said, 'Let light shine out of darkness,' has shone in our hearts to bring to light the knowledge of the glory of God on the face of [Jesus] Christ" (2 Cor 4:6).

Like Winnowed Chaff

Going out to harvest wild rice, my ricing partner and I always begin by praying the first psalm. Ricers go two to a canoe, one standing in the stern to use a long pole to push the craft through the rice stalks. The other, seated in the canoe, uses two sticks to pull the rice stalks over the canoe with one arm and beat the grains of the stalks with the other arm and stick so that they land safely in the hull.

The native people would process the harvest by drying the rice, digging a shallow hole, lining it with an animal skin, and pouring in the rice. The men, in moccasins, would dance on the grains to break their hulls. Later, the women would scoop the rice into shallow baskets, and heave it into the air. The wind would blow away the chaff, while the plump grains of *mahnomen*, the Ojibwe or Chippewa word for wild rice, would land safely in the basket. In Psalm 1, we pray that we might be similarly gathered in with the just, and not numbered among the wicked, for "[t]hey are like chaff driven by the wind." These, the wicked, might include those of whom Jesus speaks who "pay no attention to judgment and to love for God" (Luke 11:42).

We who seek the face of God are alert as Paul enumerates "the fruit of the Spirit," which ought to characterize those who belong to Christ: "love, joy, peace, patience, kindness, generosity, faithfulness, gentleness, self-control" (Gal 5:22-23).

Love Looks like What?

Saint Augustine, a bishop in northern Africa in the fourth century, is said to have asked, "What does love look like?" He offered a ready response to his own question: "It has the hands to help others. It has the feet to hasten to the poor and needy. It has eyes to see misery and want. It has the ears to hear the sighs and sorrows of men. That is what love looks like."[1]

His insight occurs to holy people in every age. At least it should. Writing in the sixteenth century, St. Teresa of Avila also observed,

> Christ has no body now but yours,
> No hands, no feet on earth but yours,
> Yours are the eyes with which he looks
> With compassion on this world,
> Yours are the feet with which he walks to do good,
> Yours are the hands, with which he blesses all the world,
> Yours are the hands, yours are the feet,
> Yours are the eyes, you are his body.
> Christ has no body now but yours,
> No hands, no feet on earth but yours,
> Yours are the eyes with which he looks
> With compassion on this world.
> Christ has no body now on earth but yours.

Such is the vision of the saints. We who would be saints must share the vision, and the commitment to compassionate care for the poor that follows.

Note

1. Lloyd Cory, *Quote, Unquote* (Wheaton, IL: Victor Books, 1977), 197.

Misery, the Call to Worship, and the Vision of Glory

Poor old Job. He called "life on earth a drudgery." But his life seemed worse than that. He lamented, "I have been assigned months of futility, / and troubled nights have been counted off for me." His insomnia sounded worse than any we might have known. He reports, "the night drags on; / I am filled with restlessness until the dawn." His "days are swifter than a weaver's shuttle" but "they come to an end without hope." He despairs, "my eye will not see happiness again" (7:1, 3, 4, 6, 7). Ouch.

The bleakness of Job's experience as we read it does not give us the promise of a happy ending. It details sorrow, woe, and a landscape that has lost sight of hope, his problems so difficult that not even God can seem to fix them if God were even to notice or care. Does it seem astonishing, then, that this bleak picture is followed immediately by the Psalms, which invite us to "sing praise to our God [who heals] the brokenhearted" (147:1, 3)? The psalmist reminds us, "Praise the Lord, for he is good" (136:1). He prompts us to recall, "The Lord rebuilds Jerusalem, / and gathers the dispersed of Israel, / Healing the brokenhearted, / and binding up their wounds." This is not a God unaware of our suffering, for "He numbers the stars, / and gives to all of them their names." This great and wise God is the God of justice; each gets what she or he deserves: "The Lord gives aid to the poor, / but casts the wicked to the ground" (147:2-3, 4, 6).

Job's suffering is not the final word. Even were his travail not to have ended happily with his family and fortune restored, he and we would still be called to lives of praise and thanksgiving. The apostle Paul puts this call to lives of worship, faithfulness, and evangelism into Christian perspective. He recognizes his call to preach the gospel and reports, "an obligation has been imposed on me, and woe to me if I do not preach it!" Why does he do all that he does? All his efforts, he writes, are "for the sake of the gospel, so that I too may have a share in it" (1 Cor 9:16, 23).

This kind of faithfulness is difficult for many of us to understand. Job did not give in to despair; he did not take his wife's advice. She gave the worst advice of any recorded anywhere in literature, telling her husband, "Curse God and die!" (2:9). But he did not. And even though he did not do so patiently, he waited for the Lord. In the end, he praised God: "I know that you can do all things, / and that no purpose of yours can be hindered. / . . . I have spoken but did not understand; / things too marvelous for me, which I did not know. / . . . By hearsay I had heard of you, / but now my eye has seen you. / Therefore I disown what I have said, / and repent in dust and ashes" (42:2-3, 5-6).

Paul, convinced of the glory of God's reign, carried the message of a hope that is beyond anything we could ask for or even imagine. This announcement of God's good reign is first made by Jesus, and at least some of his contemporaries were aware of the significance of what they heard and saw. After Jesus cured Simon's mother-in-law who had been sick with a fever, "The whole town was gathered at the door." According to Mark's report, "He cured many who were sick with various diseases" (1:33-34).

The next day, "Rising very early before dawn, he left and went off to a deserted place, where he prayed. Simon and those who were with him pursued him and on finding him said, 'Everyone is looking for you.'" (Mark 1:35-37).

This is the company to which we are called, to be part of the great crowd looking for Jesus. When we begin to understand the great promise to which we are called, even the greatest difficulties of life cannot obscure our vision. So we continue to come day by day, week by week, year by year, to the twin tables of Word and Eucharist.

My Evangelical Failure

I sent a text message recently to two college students out doing internships before their senior year of study: "I have Mass at the Basilica in Minneapolis on Sunday at 11:30. If u 2 are in town, come and I'll take u for brunch and beer afterwards." Both of them, more or less raised Catholic, immediately accepted the brunch invite but declined Mass.

I parried: it was the ninety-seventh anniversary of the dedication of the grand and historic building, the first basilica in America, designed by Emmanuel Louis Masqueray, who is renowned in American architecture; the music would be excellent, a jazz trio offering riffs on "Be Thou My Vision" bouncing about the best acoustical space around, filled to capacity with one thousand plus worshipers. And, I added humbly, "The preacher is pretty good too." In response: "Ha!"

Why would young people turn down the invitation to worship? They were not asked to go to a dark place, to participate in a dull rite, or to endure a morning of boredom. But yet there was no spark of interest in either of them even with a personal invitation pressed upon them to a grand event in an impressive place.

Here is what I will ask them: What is it about the established church that invites a bored lack of interest? Whose fault is that?

My Evangelical Failure, Part the Second

After I made the lament at the Basilica of Saint Mary in Minneapolis about the August text message to two College of St. Scholastica students ("I have Mass at the Basilica in Minneapolis on Sunday at 11:30. If u 2 are in town, come and I'll take u for brunch and beer afterwards"), I received a number of answers to my question. One thoughtful correspondent wrote, "You know quite well why they feel uncomfortable at a Catholic Mass these days, just as thousands of our young and older do. It is because of the dichotomy between the down-to-earth teachings and inclusive love of Jesus and a judgmental and exclusive understanding about who may be given access to the sacramental Body of Christ and who may actually attempt to BECOME the Body of Christ in the world today."

This correspondent also asked, "Do persons who have committed 'serious sin' feel welcome? Do women feel entirely welcome? Do divorced Catholics feel welcome? Perhaps your two young friends are in one of these groups themselves or know others who are." The writer also noted, "I am grieving the present state of our church. I continue to celebrate Mass and receive the sacraments because they are precious to me and I keep praying that the Holy Spirit who renews the face of the earth will renew the church and transform it into the compassionate face of the living Jesus who held out his arms to all on the cross and continues to hold them out to all today."

There is the key, I think: "I grieve; I continue." It seems to me that the young people who are not part of us have not wandered away; they are the children of people who have wandered away either in anger or indifference. The church is poorer for the absence of both generations; and the children are poorer not to have been raised in our rich tradition. They cannot return to something or someplace they have never known. Of all the college students I know who were raised without a church, not one has expressed gratitude to the parents for that omission. Those who remain active in this Holy Family, in our church that is at once sinful and redeemed, are the Body of Christ. Inspired by the Holy Spirit, they will transform the face of the church and the earth.

While we know next to nothing about the thirty years of Jesus' life before his baptism, except for the trip to Jerusalem when he was twelve (a trip made in observance of the law), we can expect that it was a place in which God was put first, where prayer was frequent, even habitual, where love, truth, justice, forgiveness, and forbearance were practiced. The Holy Family invites our own holy families, or not quite so holy families, to pray together, to implore the intercession of the members of the Holy Family and to imitate their virtues.

And let's remember St. Monica too; by the power of her prayer and the work of the Holy Spirit, her reprobate son, Augustine, turned out to be one of the most significant figures in Christianity.

We have opportunities, and we must take them, to study the faith. This can be especially true for folks who know their own formation to be inadequate. There is still time to learn the faith better, to live it more fully, and to pass it on in all its richness. To remain Catholic and to raise a new generation of Catholics, or to be that generation, is possible; doing so will make us holy and wise. This task requires great grace. God, without doubt, wishes to bestow that grace upon us. There are many reasons I know that this is true.

One of the reasons is that one of my students, hearing of the homily in which I lamented the absence of those two other students, sent me a note: "Father Graham, unlike the two students you mentioned, I would love to attend Mass AND meet up for brunch. The next time you are at the basilica, I will be there with a Catholic friend; we would both enjoy a quality discussion and some good food. Send me a text."

And so I did. And so we will. Only one of us is old enough to drink a beer at brunch. But still: Thanks be to God!

Nones at Christmas

The Pew Forum on Religion and Public Life tells us that some 45 million people, about one-fifth of the adults in the United States, now report that they belong to no church in particular. Of these, only 6 percent are either atheist or agnostic. So, what do all those unattached believers do at Christmas?

National Public Radio tells of "Broadway's Profit-Turning, Crowd-Pleasing Christmas Story."[1] We hear that "the Christmas season is when retailers make the bulk of their profits, Hollywood blockbusters rake it in, and Broadway theaters are filled to capacity. In recent seasons, Broadway has even staged special limited-run holiday musicals— among them, adaptations of *A Christmas Story* and *Elf*." *A Christmas Story* is not what you might think; it is a musical about growing up in Indiana. And *Elf*, well, is about an elf.

Broadway's investors have an approach they call "patience; it's one of long-term strategy . . . It's an annuity for us and our families for a few generations to come." Well, that's an approach. The reporter continues, "This new breed of holiday musical has both built-in advantages and built-in disadvantages. The advantage is they're based on well-known movie properties, so they all have name recognition; the disadvantage is it only makes sense to produce them for a couple of months around Christmastime." Perhaps there are other strategies to consider, different kinds of patience. And other kinds of disadvantages too. Where, for example, does Broadway's approach leave Isaiah the prophet:

> The people who walked in darkness
>   have seen a great light;
> Upon those who lived in a land of gloom
>   a light has shone.
> You have brought them abundant joy
>   and great rejoicing;
> They rejoice before you as people rejoice at harvest,
>   as they exult when dividing the spoils.

For the yoke that burdened them,
  the pole on their shoulder,
The rod of their taskmaster,
  you have smashed, as on the day of Midian.
For every boot that tramped in battle,
  every cloak rolled in blood,
  will be burned as fuel for fire.
For a child is born to us, a son is given to us;
  upon his shoulder dominion rests.
They name him Wonder-Counselor, God-Hero,
  Father-Forever, Prince of Peace. (9:1-5)

And what about Luke: "In those days a decree went out from Caesar Augustus that the whole world should be enrolled. This was the first enrollment, when Quirinius was governor of Syria. So all went to be enrolled, each to his own town. And Joseph too went up from Galilee from the town of Nazareth to Judea, to the city of David that is called Bethlehem, because he was of the house and family of David, to be enrolled with Mary, his betrothed, who was with child. While they were there, the time came for her to have her child, and she gave birth to her firstborn son. She wrapped him in swaddling clothes and laid him in a manger, because there was no room for them in the inn" (2:1-7).

And don't forget Charles Wesley:

Hark! The herald angels sing,
"Glory to the newborn King;
Peace on earth, and mercy mild,
God and sinners reconciled!"
Joyful, all ye nations rise,
Join the triumph of the skies;
With th' angelic host proclaim,
"Christ is born in Bethlehem!"

Perhaps here we have a double tragedy: popular culture moving ahead with tinseled themes that reflect light but not divinity; and, an evangelical opportunity that has missed almost an entire generation in a developed nation.

Note

1. Jeff Lunden, "Broadway's Profit-Turning, Crowd-Pleasing Christmas Story," December 21, 2012, http://www.npr.org/2012/12/21/167467459/broadways-profit-turning-crowd-pleasing-christmas-story.

Not to Ministering Angels

Speaking of Jesus, the author of the Letter to the Hebrews notes, "Surely he did not help angels but rather the descendants of Abraham" (2:16). That author might have been a student of the Talmud, the sacred text in Judaism that's over six thousand pages long and contains the opinions of thousands of rabbis on a variety of topics. In the Talmud, we learn, "The Torah was not given to ministering angels" (Berachot 2Sb). Then follows an often-quoted dialogue between Moses and the angels when Moses ascended on high to receive the Torah from God. Why should such a treasure be given to humanity? wondered the angels. Moses answers their question with a series of questions:

> Did you go down to Egypt? Were you enslaved to Pharaoh? Why then should the Torah be yours? . . . Do you perform work that you need the Shabbat as a day of rest? Do you have business dealings that you need a law against falsehood? Is there jealousy amongst you that you need rules against murder and theft? (Talmud, Shabbat 88b-89a)

The point is that the Torah is clearly given for imperfect beings, for those who live with all the problems of ordinary human life.

We Christians ought to also ask for whom the gospel is given. Hint: not to ministering angels.

Numbers of the Heavenly Church

I always wake up on All Saints' Day especially glad to be a Catholic, secure in our tradition of reading the Bible as sometimes literal and sometimes figurative, symbolic, always challenging, the enduring Word in every season. On All Saints' Day, we read from the book of Revelation (7:2-4, 9-14); these passages must be frightening to hear in traditions that regard this final book of the Bible as literally true. Happily, I think, we Catholics, along with the Orthodox, Episcopalians, and most mainline Protestants, distinguish between the literal and the figurative language of the Scriptures. For example, "I heard the number of those who had been marked with the seal, one hundred and forty-four thousand . . . " (7:4). To some literal readers of the Bible, this means that there will be room for only 144,000 people in heaven. Yikes! That would only be room for the monks of Saint John's in Collegeville, their families, and former students. What about Notre Dame? And the rest of us in all God's world?

Some go so far as to assert that "the final number of the heavenly church will be 144,000, according to God's decree."[1] As we read the same text, however, "The number is obviously symbolic. Twelve (the number of the tribes) is both squared and multiplied by 1,000—a twofold way of emphasizing completeness."[2] As we read the gospel (see Matt 5:1-12a), we see God's house as ready to accommodate all who seek entry. The first Eucharistic Prayer for Reconciliation in *The Roman Missal* gives us an extraordinary vision of the communion of saints to which we aspire. As we pray, we anticipate the hour when we will stand before God: "Saints among the Saints in the halls of heaven." The second Eucharistic Prayer for Reconciliation amplifies that vision, anticipating the heaven's banquet of unity "in a new heaven and a new earth" where the fullness of God's peace will shine. There will be gathered Mary, the apostles, all the saints, "with our brothers and sisters / and those of every race and tongue / who have died" in God's friendship. Note that our prayer leaves it to God to decide who has died in divine friendship.

The tapestries that hang in the Cathedral of Our Lady of the Angels in Los Angeles offer a broad, wonderful, and inclusive example of a vision of the communion of saints to which the feast of All Saints calls us. Twenty-five large and long tapestries around the nave of the cathedral show 135 saints from around the world. Among them are the canonized women and men of North America. There are also twelve untitled figures, including children of different ages, who are to suggest the unknown holy people in our midst. Included are people of every age, race, occupation, and vocation. Especially wonderful is that saints from the Middle Ages mingle with people from the first and the twentieth centuries. I think that St. Felicity, from second-century Rome, stands next to or near St. John Baptist de La Salle of seventeenth-century France. All of them face the light of the great cross-window above the altar where the Eucharist is celebrated. Our gaze is to follow theirs. The figures are above our heads and call to mind the words of William Walsham How's 1864 hymn sung often on this feast, "For All the Saints." The hymn envisions, "O blest communion, fellowship divine! / we feebly struggle, they in glory shine; / all are one in thee, for all are thine. / Alleluia, Alleluia!"

This is the communion to which Jesus calls us, and which is nourished at the twin tables of Word and bread. In the Beatitudes, Jesus tells us about saintly happiness, how to seek it, how to cultivate it, and where it will come to fulfillment. We wait and long in joyful hope for the reward that will be great in heaven, knowing that "we are God's children now; / what we shall be has not yet been revealed" (1 John 3:2).

Notes

1. *Let God Be True*, rev. ed. (Brooklyn, NY: Watch Tower Bible and Tract Society, 1952), 130.

2. Robert Mounce, *The Book of Revelation* (Grand Rapids: Eerdmans, 1977), 168.

Our Father

Jesus said to his disciples, "This is how you are to pray." And he begins, "Our Father, who art in heaven." For Jesus to call God Father, or *Abba*, was daring in its informality. When we say "Our Father," God becomes accessible in a new and personal way, and God's love is revealed as unconditional. When we dare to call God "Father," we open ourselves to this relationship that really does extend to us. We embrace the good news that in Jesus we are offered divine life. God is now Father to us; we accept the gift of becoming God's children.

In his nineteenth-century paraphrase of Psalm 102 (103), hymn writer Henry F. Lyte wrote, "Father-like he tends and spares us; Well our feeble frame he knows; In his hands he gently bears us, Rescues us from all our foes. Alleluia! Alleluia! Widely yet his mercy flows." This is the God who is "Slow to chide, and swift to bless," and "Glorious is his faithfulness." We may sense an even deeper, more radical claim in Jesus' use, and our own, of *Abba*, and a broader, more inclusive sense of God. We have to dare to say it, to call on God as if children in the night. We must be "formed by the Word" before we really express this relationship, claiming it boldly.

Out of the Mouths of Babes

Out of the mouths of infants and nurslings you have brought forth praise.

— Matthew 21:16

Before the 9:30 Mass one Sunday at the Basilica of Saint Mary in Minneapolis, I donned alb, stole, chasuble, and microphone and spent some minutes outside greeting arriving worshipers, then went in and found a seat in the back pew so I could listen to the organ prelude by one of Minnesota's best organists on one of Minnesota's best instruments in one of Minnesota's finest worship spaces. This was to be followed by the cantor chanting the introit verse in Latin. I looked forward to some prayerful moments of preparation before Mass. As soon as I settled in, a little boy in the pew immediately in front of me turned around and, standing on the pew, eyeballed me. "Are you the priest?" he asked. "I am," I said. "Why are you back here then?" he inquired. I told him about the organ and the introit. He was not interested in either of them. He let me know that he had some questions. He was, he reported, three years old, and showed me his backpack filled with toys and books in case the church service was long. His little brother Noah, who is just one, was down the pew with mom and dad.

"What's that?" he asked, pointing to clouds of burning incense billowing from the thurible carried by the thurifer. "That," I said, "is holy smoke. As our prayers, it rises up to God." "And what's that?" he asked, pointing to the processional cross carried by the crucifer. "That is Jesus. On the cross," I answered. "And what's that?" he asked, pointing to the candles and candle bearers. "Candles. Light. Jesus," I answered. "And what's that?" he asked, pointing to the gospel book carried by the lector. "The gospel stories. More Jesus," I answered. The kid understood metaphor: cross, candles, and gospels, the multiple presences of Christ among us.

We stood to sing the opening hymn. The boy was in his father's arms to get a better view. We were still eyeball-to-eyeball. I scooped some of the incense smoke from the air and blessed us both. "Let's bow when the cross goes by," I told him. "Why?" he asked. "Jesus," I said. We bowed together. "And let's bow again when the gospel book goes by," I suggested. "Why?" he asked again. "More Jesus," I told him. We bowed again. It was my turn to join the procession. I took a few steps first toward the baptismal font, scooped out some water, brought it to the boy and blessed him, and then signed myself. I never did hear either a note of the prelude or a word of the introit, but I have rarely felt better prepared to pray.

Pagan Babies

We no longer ransom pagan babies. That might be a pity. We Catholics of a certain age did ransom them when we were young. We would skimp on our milk money, do chores around the house, mow a neighbor's lawn or shovel their snowy walk, and we would have pennies and nickels and dimes, rarely a quarter, that we were encouraged to share. A child who had a clever mechanical bank might bring it to class, and Sister would invite him to go up and down the aisle collecting our donations, and the next day, choose a classmate to make the trip again.

It seems so terribly and politically incorrect now even to use the term, much less promote the activity. We often fail to put our criticism of past efforts in their proper context. To ransom pagan babies did not mean spiriting them away from their parents and communities to be raised as Catholics in an orphanage where their souls would be saved. It meant instead to cooperate with and fund what we then called the Bishops' Relief, now more properly called the Catholic Relief Services, so that our souls could be saved. As far as their souls went, we always counted on God, as our prayers now make explicit, to "give kind admittance" to the kingdom to all who pleased God "at their passing from this life" (Eucharistic Prayer III). Our childhood efforts helped feed and clothe children in distant lands; we were encouraged along the way to recognize diversity and commonality, their place and our place, together in the reign of God, pagans and non-Catholics and Catholics alike. In God's house, there are many dwelling places (see John 14:2); we knew that even when the church's discourse did not seem to articulate it well.

Our public school friends would trick-or-treat for UNICEF; they too were encouraged to think globally even before that descriptive phrase was coined.

We may not teach our children about pagan babies these days, but if we do not create in them and model for them compassionate hearts, then we will have failed to do our duty.

Perfecting Love and Heartfelt Compassion

The apostle Paul gives evidence that he did not attempt, in his epistle to the Ephesians, to suggest how society ought to be structured always and everywhere. He writes, "Slaves, be obedient to your human masters with fear and trembling, in sincerity of heart, as to Christ" (6:5). No reasonable person would suggest that Paul thought slavery was either a good idea or an example to the church in every age. Instead, we see here Paul's understanding of the immanent coming of Christ. It is clear in Paul's writing that he expected the second coming of Christ to be soon, very soon, perhaps even in his own lifetime. Preparing for the coming of the Messiah was a task to be undertaken with urgency. Social restructuring and other tasks ceased to be important, especially since they could not be accomplished before the return of the Lord. Since the bridegroom has been long delayed (see Matt 25:5), we have come to understand that the teaching of Jesus and the message of Christian salvation applies to society, economic life, and social institutions as well as to individuals.[1]

Still, in present circumstances, each ought to live the life of Christ, in perfecting love and heartfelt compassion. It is in this way that, as did the earliest Christians, we too "Strive to enter through the narrow door" (Luke 13:24).

Note

1. See, for example, Josiah Strong, *Our Country: Its Possible Future and Its Current Crisis* (New York: The American Home Missionary Society, 1885).

Peter's Chair

The idea of a feast called the Chair of Saint Peter, which we celebrate on February 22, may sound a bit odd in our English language. One might wonder what is particularly to be celebrated about a chair. But if we frame the consideration by beginning with the Latin word for chair, *cathedra*, the feast seems not just sensible, but significant.

The *cathedra* is found in the cathedral; both the chair and that particular church building house the bishop. And the bishop, who is the chief teacher, speaks authoritatively from that chair. Thus the Chair of Peter suggests to us the unifying office of the Bishop of Rome, traditionally esteemed as the successor of Peter the apostle. Each bishop is a successor of the apostles, but only the Bishop of Rome is the successor of a particular apostle. This bishop, the servant of the servants of God, is the *Pontifex Maximus*, which we usually understand as the high priest, but a literal translation is Greatest Bridge Builder. So the pope, as the bishop of bishops, has as his great responsibility to unite all the local churches by the building of bridges. Thus he is to be, as we read in the First Letter of Peter, an example to the flock.

We pray always that our current pope may have the inspired vision of Peter the apostle who, though not always strong or heroic in the gospels, was the first to recognize that Jesus was more than an inspired teacher. His faith prompts him to profess, "You are the Messiah, the Son of the living God" (Matt 16:16). May our faith echo that of faithful Peter.

Phyllis

I got an e-mail from Arlene, a member of a parish of which I was once the pastor. She wrote, "I visit and bring communion to Phyllis. On Wednesday, she was very upset and concerned that she might have sinned. She has been quite worried. One of her caregivers thought a priest should visit her. She recently had her 103rd birthday! Let me know what you think." "Well," I wrote back, "Anne had mentioned Phyllis to me this week, too, so I have been thinking of her and will surely visit right away." I added, "I look forward to seeing her, and feel pretty confident that any sins she may be committing are small."

It is a good chance that her sins indeed are small, but she has also been clearly and richly formed by her life as a faithful Catholic. She has heard the voice of the apostle Paul as we have heard it ourselves in his Letter to the Colossians: God "has now reconciled [you] . . . to present you holy, without blemish, and irreproachable before him." Phyllis has persevered "in the faith," is "firmly grounded, stable," and has not shifted "from the hope of the gospel" that she has heard all these 103 years (Col 1:22-23). She knows in her heart and in her bones what we acclaim, using the words of Jesus himself: "I am the way and the truth and the life. No one comes to the Father except through me" (John 14:6).

So, God bless Phyllis for more than a century of faithful living with her sins confessed and forgiven. And, blessings on Anne and Arlene. May their compassionate hearts find rest in the Jesus they imitate!

Plumber's Butt: Two Views

I was in Albuquerque not so long ago and had dinner with friends at a Brazilian restaurant that attracted a young crowd. Seated near us was a large group of twenty-somethings having a lively time. One of their members was a large young man who could have safely sought out a larger pant size. His display of his posterior was expansive, and inescapable from my table without a very strict application of what we used to call custody of the eyes.

There are two ways to view the view that he offered. First, one might adopt one of the rallying cries of the 1960s: Let it all hang out. One might also say, Embrace the reality of who you are.

Or, on second thought, one might consider, See yourself as others see you.

No one can really want to display a plumber's butt either literally or metaphorically. Folks might see in us what we do not see, or a facet of our personality that we are unaware of, or at least unaware of how it is perceived by others.

One of the prefaces in the Missal asks that the Father "might love in us what you loved in your Son" (Ordinary Time VII). While we count on God to embrace the whole of our person, parts of our person, both physical and spiritual, may need attention as we continue the practice of *metanoia*, the change of our hearts and minds and attitudes.

Saints, and those who would be saints, come in all shapes and pant sizes. But, we, all of us, might pull up those pants and tighten our belts, and get on with the matters at hand. Or, as St. Benedict puts it in his Prologue of the Rule for monasteries, "Clothed then with faith and the performance of good works, let us set out on this way, with the Gospel for our guide, that we may deserve to see him *who has called us to his kingdom* (1 Thess 2:12)" (21).

Polished Arrows, Hidden Quiver: Showing in Our Lives the Glory of God

I hired a bright, young, recent college graduate to give me a hand with some summer tasks before he went off to graduate school in the fall. On the first day of summer, we devoted ourselves to painting and (late) spring cleaning. At noon, I took him to our local diner out at Four Corners in Canosia Township. We entered, seated ourselves, and were greeted in a heartbeat by an attractive young waitress who introduced herself by name. While she spoke to both of us, she looked only at my young companion. He is a sturdy young man with an engaging smile. She, lovely and vibrant, is perhaps seventeen or eighteen years old. The object of her gaze is twenty-two, an older man.

Had I not been so taken by her attention to the object of her stares, I would have felt a bit insulted at having been rendered invisible. She returned so often to our table, floating over to stand close to him, that I finally asked my young friend if he was aware of the chemical reaction that his very presence had occasioned.

He nodded and smiled. She returned. He flirted; she giggled. I remained invisible. She thought he should have dessert. He asked what she would recommend. She recited the list of her favorites and said he could safely choose any of them. I visited the men's room; she came back to see him twice in the minutes I was away. Paying the check, I tipped her generously for what I knew would soon work itself into either a homily or a reflective article.

Our first attraction to people is by their looks. He knew that. So did she. But looks can deceive. Character cannot. Both of them can expect to have long lives ahead, but could squander or abuse their gifts and other people, later seeing themselves as the prophet Isaiah first saw himself: "I thought I had toiled in vain, / for nothing and for naught spent my strength" (49:4). This young woman revealed herself as interested, innocent, and vulnerable. He revealed himself as kind and gracious. Many people move from this kind of beginning to disaster.

I hope she will not, though I do not remember her name or know anything about her. I trust that he will not move to disaster. May God call them both to become like Isaiah whom God called by name from his mother's womb. Isaiah reports that God "made my mouth like a sharp-edged sword, / concealed me, shielded by his hand. / He made me a sharpened arrow, / in his quiver he hid me. / He said to me, You are my servant, / in you, Israel, I show my glory" (49:2-3).

What a glorious vocation: to show in our own lives the glory of God. Calling Isaiah to this vocation, God speaks: "It is too little, he says, for you to be my servant, / to raise up the tribes of Jacob, / and restore the survivors of Israel; / I will make you a light to the nations, / that my salvation may reach to the ends of the earth" (49:6).

The church employs Isaiah's words to speak of John the Baptizer, a giant in our tradition. John, the forerunner of Jesus, announced the light that brings salvation to all the world. Remember Luke's account of the visitation: "When Elizabeth heard Mary's greeting, the infant leaped in her womb." Elizabeth, pregnant with John the Baptist, later tells Mary, pregnant with Jesus, "For at the moment the sound of your greeting reached my ears, the infant in my womb leaped for joy" (1:41, 44). John was about his task of announcing the coming of the Messiah even before his birth. Perhaps we can and should see the kind young man and lovely young woman, and ourselves too, in John's same tradition. We must then convince ourselves that joy, holiness, and wholesomeness are in fact far more common than we might first think. John Paul II clearly thought this in promoting so many as saints. If they can be holy, we can be holy. We too can announce the light that brings salvation to all the world, showing in our own lives the glory of God.

Is this not the best gift of the developing church to all of society: the sending forth of women and men who have learned in the school of the Lord's service, shaped into the polished arrow hidden in God's quiver of which Isaiah sang?

The dean of the School of Arts and Letters at the college where I once taught, Dr. Tammy Ostrander, responded to one of my recent notes with a quote from Isaiah: "Perhaps," she wrote, "I can make the rough places plain and the crooked places straight." This piece of Isaiah's job description is the vision for a Catholic college, and a mission statement for all in the Body of Christ.

We in the church are in the business of salvation, and all our efforts are directed to the pursuit of truth, and to moving and touching hearts. Saint John Baptist de La Salle, founder of the Christian Brothers, writes that "God wills not only that all come to the knowledge of truth, but also that all be saved."[1] According to de La Salle, procuring salvation meant seeking the total well-being of each student, and this process would begin with the teacher seeking to touch the hearts of the students entrusted to him. He speaks to each of us when he writes, "You carry out a work that requires you to touch hearts, but this you cannot do except by the Spirit of God."

Father Timothy Radcliffe, the former master general of the Dominican Order, writes in *Liturgy in a Postmodern World* that the preacher today must do what Jesus did at the Last Supper. Every baptized person, I think, shares this same task defined by Radcliffe: "1. Jesus reaches out to his disciples in their individual puzzlement and confusion; 2. He gathers them into community; 3. He reaches beyond this community for the fullness of the Kingdom."[2] This is a prophetic task. We trust that God will continue to raise up prophets in every age; their power in our midst will make us ready to receive with joy the one whom we announce.

Notes

1. John Baptist de La Salle, *Meditations for the Time of Retreat*, in *John Baptist de la Salle: The Spirituality of Chrsitian Education*, ed. Carl Koch, Jeffrey Calligan, and Jeffrey Gros (Mahwah, NJ: Paulist Press, 2004), 39

2. Timothy Radcliffe, *Liturgy in a Postmodern World*, ed. Keith F. Pecklers (New York: Continuum, 2003), 135.

Power

In our church and in our society today, we are acutely sensitive to both the arrogance of power and the abuse of power. But for an example of a higher understanding and better use of power, think of Jesus, tempted in the wilderness. He does not turn stones to bread to satisfy his hunger because the power of Jesus is used always on behalf of others, never to satisfy personal need or desire.

I was helped to recognize this Lenten lesson by an e-mail one of my sisters sent out not so long ago; it is a story making the rounds on the internet so others may have the same story.

An officer of the Drug Enforcement Administration stopped at a ranch in Texas and spoke with an old rancher. He told the rancher, "I need to inspect your ranch for illegally grown drugs." The rancher said, "Okay, but don't go in that field over there," as he pointed out the location.

The DEA officer exploded, saying, "Mister, I have the authority of the Federal Government with me." Reaching into his rear pants pocket, he removed his badge and proudly displayed it to the rancher. "See this badge? This badge means I am allowed to go wherever I wish. On any land. No questions asked or answers given. Have I made myself clear? Do you understand?"

The rancher nodded politely, apologized, and went about his chores. A short time later, the old rancher heard loud screams and saw the DEA officer running for his life chased by the rancher's enormous bull.

With every step the bull was gaining ground on the officer, and it seemed likely that he'd be gored before he reached safety. The officer was clearly terrified. The rancher threw down his tools, ran to the fence and yelled loudly: "Your badge! Show him your badge!"

Profitably Practicing Lent

In our annual observance of Lent, we prepare by works of charity and self-sacrifice to renew our baptismal promises, recommitting ourselves to the mystery, reconfiguring ourselves to Christ, seeking to conform ourselves to the Word who moves among us for our salvation. And if we keep doing what we are supposed to be doing, at some point, we will be happy in the presence of God. Leo the Great observes that "with the return of the season marked out in a special way by the mystery of our redemption, and of the days that lead up to the paschal feast, we are summoned more urgently to prepare ourselves by a purification of spirit." The special note of the paschal feast is, he writes, that "the whole Church rejoices in the forgiveness of sins." So, "what the Christian should be doing at all times should now be done with greater care and devotion, so that the Lenten fast enjoined by the apostles may be fulfilled, not simply by abstinence from food but above all by the renunciation of sin." And "there is no more profitable practice as a companion to holy and spiritual fasting than that of almsgiving." Under "the single name of mercy" are embraced "many excellent works of devotion." Thus "the person who shows love and compassion to those in any kind of affliction is blessed, not only with the virtue of good will but also with the gift of peace."[1]

To recognize that we desire such peace is the first step on the path to peace. Or, as a freshman student, Philip, explained to me, "The attempt to love your neighbors as yourself is said to be the path of perfection. I've known at a young age to respect others but I have not fully reached my understanding or willingness to do so." Lent is for us an opportunity to embrace such struggles as Philip sees. In the struggle, we claim the power of the Spirit given to us in the baptismal waters. This Spirit keeps alive the memory of Jesus in our hearts and minds so that we can attend with all alacrity to Paul's prompt: "But what does [Scripture] say? / "The word is near you, / in your mouth and in your heart" / (that is, the word of faith that we preach), for, if you confess with your mouth that Jesus is Lord and believe in your heart that God raised him from the dead, you will be saved" (Rom 10:8-9).

Ruth, another student hard at work thinking theologically, asked, "If we confess and believe that Jesus is Lord, should we then not somehow look or behave differently?" Yes. Isaiah the prophet, I think, anticipated her wise question when, with the voice of God, he enumerated the wishes of God: "Is this not, rather, the fast that I choose: / releasing those bound unjustly, / untying the thongs of the yoke; / Setting free the oppressed, / breaking off every yoke? / Is it not sharing your bread with the hungry, / bringing the afflicted and the homeless into your house; / Clothing the naked when you see them, / and not turning your back on your own flesh?" (58:6-7). When we do these things, we are transformed; as we lighten the burdens of those who suffer or who are oppressed in any way, we come a step closer to the fullness of God's reign. And then, "your light shall break forth like the dawn, / and your wound shall quickly be healed; / Your vindication shall go before you, / and the glory of the LORD shall be your rear guard. / Then you shall call, and the LORD will answer, / you shall cry for help, and he will say: Here I am!" (58:8-9a).

So we who live in the Holy Spirit and in the church hope to share in God's glory. We look to Jesus, the pioneer and the perfecter of our faith. By reflecting on Jesus, we get a picture of what kinds of persons we should strive to become. In our Lenten practices, and when we fast, we will sharpen our hunger for God and commit ourselves to acting on behalf of those who do not have enough. Our Lenten practices call us to seek God in those who suffer.

So what kind of a season is Lent? The first Lenten preface to the eucharistic prayer in the Roman Missal says to God, "For by your gracious gift each year / your faithful await the sacred paschal feasts / with the joy of minds made pure." What will a proper observance of Lent do for us? The preface says confidently to God, by "participating in the mysteries / by which [we] have been reborn, / [we] may be led to the fullness of grace / that you bestow on your sons and daughters." And the collect of Lent's first Sunday asks the Father, "through the yearly observances of holy Lent, / that we may grow in understanding / of the riches hidden in Christ / and by worthy conduct pursue their effects." And on the fourth Sunday, in the collect, we ask "that with prompt devotion and eager faith / the Christian people may hasten / toward the solemn celebrations to come." Soon, then, we will recognize what St. Cyril of Jerusalem meant when he instructed the catechumens: "The goal set before us is no trifling one; we are striving for eternal life."[2]

Notes

1. Leo the Great, qtd. in *The Liturgy of the Hours*, vol. 2 (New York: Catholic Book Publishing, 1975), 60–61.

2. Cyril of Jerusalem, catechetical instruction, qtd. in *The Liturgy of the Hours*, vol. 3 (New York: Catholic Book Publishing, 1975), 561.

Reconciling Power in the Church

Paul tells us, "You were dead in your transgressions and sins in which you once lived following the age of this world . . . For by grace you have been saved through faith" (Eph 2:1, 8). Bringing us from death to life is the great gift of the Creator. Pope St. Leo the Great, in the fifth century, suggested how we might receive this gift; he admonished, "Christian, remember your dignity, and now that you share in God's own nature, do not return by sin to your former base condition. Bear in mind who is your head and of whose body you are a member. Do not forget that you have been rescued from the power of darkness and brought into the light of God's kingdom."[1]

Seeking the light, we pray with the psalmist, "The LORD is God, / he made us, we belong to him" (100:3). And we attend carefully to the call of Jesus as we seek to be "rich in what matters to God" (Luke 12:21). The kind of transformation of hearts, minds, and attitudes to which we are called is enabled by the sacrament of reconciliation. We do well to "acknowledge our sins," as we do at each Eucharist. We also do well to confess our sins regularly so that we might even better know and experience the tenderness of God and the reconciling power that is in our church. Thanks be to God.

Note

1. Pope Leo the Great, Sermon 1, *Nativitate Domini*, qtd. in *The Liturgy of the Hours*, vol. 1 (New York: Catholic Book Publishing, 1975), 404–5.

Ritual as Teacher

I recently dipped a newborn into the baptismal waters. She was lifted up, dried off, anointed with chrism announcing her royal status, and dressed in the finery befitting her status as a daughter of God. Then, for some reason, her godfather leaned over to me and whispered conspiratorially, "I used to be an altar boy, Father, so let me know if you need any help." I smiled, thanked him, handed him the baptismal candle, and pointed to the paschal candle; he knew immediately to light hers from the Light of Christ. He thought, perhaps, that he had helped. He had only just begun. The ritual admonition that followed outlined the help that he was called to give. But it was not an altar boy's assistance, nor was it help to the baptizing priest. After the candle has been lighted, the minister speaks:

> Parents and godparents, this light is entrusted to you to be kept burning brightly. This child of yours has been enlightened by Christ. She is to walk always as a child of the light. May she keep the flame of faith alive in her heart. When the Lord comes, may she go out to meet him with all the saints in the heavenly kingdom. (Explanatory Rites 100, Rite of Baptism for Children)

These parents and godparents, having answered affirmatively when asked, "Is it your will that this child should be baptized in the faith of the Church, which we have all professed with you?" were undertaking to "bring her up in the practice of the faith . . . see[ing] that the divine life which God gives her is kept safe from the poison of sin, to grow always stronger in her heart" (97, 93).

God's grace and the church's assistance are offered to the parents and godparents in their awesome responsibilities, as the final blessing suggests: "By God's gift, through water and the Holy Spirit, we are reborn to everlasting life. In his goodness, may he continue to pour out his blessings upon these sons and daughters of his. May he make them always, wherever they may be, faithful members of his holy people" (105).

The parents and godparents have quite some task ahead of them, one to be shared by all the church. It takes a village to seek the kingdom of God, one could say. And what we were about in that ritual moment was well explained by the rite itself; how cool is that?

Sabbath Sentiments:
Awe in the Presence of Majesty

On the seventh day God completed the work he had been doing;
he rested on the seventh day from all the work he had undertaken.
God blessed the seventh day and made it holy,
because on it he rested from all the work he had done in creation.

— Genesis 2:2-3

Blessed are they that shop on the Sabbath,
For they shall get the best bargains.
Oh, yes, this is a very fine country.

— The Devil, speaking in *The Testament of Gideon Mack*, a novel by James Robertson

I was chatting with a student one morning when Sister Marilyn walked by in the college corridor on a foray from the monastery next door. I introduced him to her and noted that she had been the principal of St. Rose School in Proctor, Minnesota, when I was a boy, back in the day before zip codes were invented. He considers me an antique (which is to say old enough to be his father), so was completely in awe of her even greater antiquity. He was far too polite to say, "Wow!" or ask, "How old are you anyway?" but simply gulped, greeted her, and stared in reverential awe. His posture at that meeting was a perfect Sabbath moment: as did God on the seventh day of creation, young David stood in awe and wonder at what the Lord had done; his open mouth and respectful greeting were, I think, an imitation of God on day seven of creation. This Sabbath posture is not inactivity. It is not just a slacker's open mouth. It is true awe in the presence of majesty. God's own creative genius is the model.

121

Perhaps we misunderstand Genesis: "On the seventh day God completed the work he had been doing; he rested on the seventh day from all the work he had undertaken. God blessed the seventh day and made it holy, because on it he rested from all the work he had done in creation" (2:2-3). Clearly, Genesis inspires us to recognize the handiwork of God with awe and wonder. In imitation and praise of the Creator, we reflect on and rejoice in the gifts that are ours to share. This rest, this true leisure, is an invitation to grace. But we are rarely able to participate in this kind of refreshing, rejuvenating activity while earning a living, attending to ledgers, managing accounts, attending to the details of careers and obligations. And that is somehow a pity.

Sabbath Sentiments II:
Is Sunday (and Are We) in Jeopardy?

Benedict XVI seems to fear that we might lose the Sabbath: "I find it extremely worrying that modern liturgists want to dismiss this social function of Sunday as a Constantinian aberration, despite the fact that it stands in continuity with the Torah of Israel."[1] Reviewing the book in *America*, Gerald O'Collins, SJ, writes, "Evidently there are a few liturgical scholars who think that, but I have never heard or read a liturgist who defends this misguided view."[2]

Perhaps no liturgist would defend that misguided view. But scores of Kmart shoppers who seek out Bluelight specials rather than take a Sunday drive or stroll seem to confuse shopping for Tide and Hanes underwear with true leisure. They give evidence that Benedict's concern might be not so much about what scholars theorize as about what Christians do on Sundays other than contemplate with awe and wonder what the Lord has done.

The *Catechism of the Catholic Church*[3] makes clear reference to the issues involved in a proper observance of Sunday or a Sabbath rest:

> God's action is the model for human action. If God "rested and was refreshed" on the seventh day, man too ought to "rest" and should let others, especially the poor, "be refreshed" [Ex 31:17; cf. 23:12]. The sabbath brings everyday work to a halt and provides a respite. It is a day of protest against the servitude of work and the worship of money [Cf. Neh 13:15-22; 2 Chr 36:21]. (CCC 2172)

Further, the *Catechism*, referencing the seventh day and God's activity (Gen 2:2), notes that "human life has a rhythm of work and rest. The institution of the Lord's Day helps everyone enjoy adequate rest and leisure to cultivate their familial, cultural, social, and religious lives [Cf. GS 67 # 3]" (2184).

So, what ought to be the activities and attitudes that suggest proper attention to the mystery of the Sabbath? Again, the *Catechism* speaks clearly: "On Sundays and other holy days of obligation, the faithful are to refrain from engaging in work or activities that hinder the worship owed to God, the joy proper to the Lord's Day, the performance of the works of mercy, and the appropriate relaxation of mind and body [Cf. CIC, can. 1247]" (2185).

These invitations are not to inactivity, indolence, or indulgence. Instead, they call us to a reverential posture, which imitates God's own pleasure in the wonderful work of the divine hand. Remember, the Spirit of God swept over the chaos as God called creation into being (Gen 1:2-3). As we are called to newness and fullness of life, that same Spirit who once hovered over the deep hovers still, assisting us to make a rich tapestry from the chaos of the strands of our lives. Sunday might then be viewed as the foretaste and promise of the paschal feast of heaven, a day to "be lived as the day of our deliverance which lets us share in this 'festal gathering,' this 'assembly of the firstborn who are enrolled in heaven' [Heb 12:22-23]" (*Catechism* 2188).

Notes

1. Joseph Ratzinger, *Jesus of Nazareth: From the Baptism in the Jordan to the Transfiguration*, trans. Adrian J. Walker (New York: Doubleday, 2007), 112.

2. Gerald O'Collins, SJ, "He Who Is," *America* (June 4, 2007).

3. *Catechism of the Catholic Church*, 2nd ed. (Libreria Editrice Vaticana, 1997).

Sabbath Sentiments III: What Should Sunday Look Like?

The prayer that accompanies the laying on of hands in the sacrament of confirmation enumerates the gifts of the Holy Spirit, our "helper and guide." These gifts include "the spirit of wisdom and understanding, / the spirit of right judgment and courage, / the spirit of knowledge and reverence / [and] . . . the spirit of wonder and awe" in God's presence (Rite of Confirmation 25). The final gift of wonder and awe has sometimes been rendered as fear of the Lord, but the current translation certainly conveys a far richer sense. Surely it is the Spirit's gift of awe and wonder that invites us to the Sabbath observance.

Tilden Edwards asserts, "Authentic sabbath time implies *freedom* and invites fresh eyes and fresh breath with which to see and be in the world." Free from the "narrow sight and limits of workaday living," we are saved from the temptations that "paralyze our responsiveness to the Spirit's presence." We then "are free to realize our fuller humanity in the image of God that is beyond our productivity." We are not then "ceaselessly toiling beasts of burden," but people who "have intrinsic value rather than merely utilitarian worth." Thus "we are free for a deeper quality of community." This worth extends to the earth as well, "where in sabbath time we do not seek to look at nature's usefulness, but rather its beauty" while we are "appreciatively present."[1]

Such an approach infiltrates our daily lives so that "we carry with us some sense of a fuller humanity that maintains our dignity and promise both alone and together, beneath and through whatever work and relationships may engulf us." In a culture more appreciative of multitasking than being at true leisure, Sabbath rest can be seen as a revolutionary act, as revolutionary tranquility. To stop "anxious productivity for a special time challenges the assumptions of a culture that would reduce us to production machines." Edwards suggests that the playful edge produced by Sabbath rest loosens the drive of our culture toward material wealth. We will then know interior wealth that leaves us full and overflowing rather than the "material wealth that in itself leaves us empty and fearful of loss."[2]

We must be aware of the fact that our technological culture can enslave us unless we call a halt. One of my young students, bright and energetic, confided to me one Lenten day that he had given up video games. Because fascination with such games is almost unimaginable to me, I had to listen closely to what his new discipline was all about. Freed from the tyranny of hours on end at controls and monitor, he found new time to delight in his tiny son, blooming marriage, wonder in abundance at every turn. His discipline, aimed at *metanoia* and new life, freed him not just from an enslavement to play that had become pointless work, but opened his eyes to real play, true joy, and honest simplicity, all of which, he could then realize, reveal the Creator's genius.

Such Sabbath times call an intentional halt to some forms of activity to make room for other pursuits or heightened awareness, making room for poetry and other arts. It is time, as Edwards puts it, "to appreciate a tree, your neighbor, and yourself without doing something to them; a time to praise God as an end in itself." I observed another young student very attentive to learning to pray the Liturgy of the Hours. He'd stop at midday to squeeze in a bit of prayer, but when I invited him to Vespers with the monastic community on campus, he begged off because "it takes so long." Sabbath posture allows time for prayer that others might regard as wasted. Instead, we see such time in prayer or in wonder as "overflowing the merely necessary," relaxing the "mental reins that would drive us to dominate our neighbor and the world." Thus we are freed "from such madness so that our appreciative mind can emerge, with its simplicity and sense of God's end-in-itself presence."[3]

Notes

1. Tilden Edwards, *Sabbath Time* (Nashville: Upper Room, 1992), 87.
2. Ibid., 88.
3. Ibid., 90.

Sabbath Sentiments IV: Sabbath Process Reveals Sabbath Posture

All we need is to experience what we already possess.

— Thomas Merton

Saint Basil the Great (330–79) asserts, "Tranquility is indeed the first step in the process of our sanctification."[1] Such tranquility is the heart, the very essence, of the Sabbath. Tilden Edwards suggests that the Sabbath "expresses the heart of the Good News, that God in Christ reveals an infinite love for us that does not depend on our works." This love depends instead "on our willingness for it, on our desire to turn to that Great Love with our deepest love, through all our little loves." Such a posture "can reveal the Gospel to our neighbors in a demonstrable, non-aggressive, yet very challenging way."[2]

Theophan the Recluse (1815–94), a Russian Orthodox monk and saint, reminds us that "the grace of God will not act on its own, but will instead await your decision." If we do not choose grace, "then it will abandon you completely, and leave you in the hands of your self will."[3] Choosing grace, we acknowledge with Bernard of Clairvaux (1090–1153, a Cistercian abbot, saint, and theologian) that God "creates minds to share in himself, gives them life, so that they may experience him, causes them to desire him, enlarges them to grasp him, justifies them so that they may deserve him, stirs them to zeal, ripens them to fruition, directs them to equity, forms them in benevolence, moderates them to make them wise, strengthens them to virtue visits them to console, enlightens them with knowledge, sustains them to immortality, fills them with happiness, surrounds them with safety."[4] So, according to Thomas Merton (1915–68), "All we need is to experience what we already possess."[5]

The simple truth is that to desire a Sabbath posture is the beginning of living that posture; the first part of the journey is the most difficult:

wanting to come to this new life. Persevering with Sabbath attitudes and practices is not easy. But a firm will is sure to yield rich results. We might approach the Sabbath as Merton suggests approaching contemplation: We must "decide where we stand and become more clear about it. That's enough." This recognition, he suggests, "is the heart of contemplative life," understanding "that you don't need any more than the real essentials." When you are "content with having met up with the essentials insofar as you can," and to "know you can't do much more than that but you've done that, is central to our life. God will take care of the rest." He points out that "suffering in the contemplative life or any religious life comes from the conviction that the action is someplace else."[6]

As Merton sees it, "living a contemplative, disciplined life should help us see what's artificial."[7] Recognizing what is artificial, we ought then to see that which is real. That which is real will endure, and "whoever endures to the end will be saved" (Matt 10:22).

Notes

1. Quoted in Lorraine Kisly, ed., *Ordinary Graces: Christian Teachings on the Interior Life* (New York: Bell Tower, 2000), 196.
2. Tilden Edwards, *Sabbath Time* (Nashville: Upper Room, 1992), 91.
3. Quoted in Kisly, *Ordinary Graces*, 82.
4. Ibid., 95.
5. Ibid., 198.
6. Thomas Merton, *The Springs of Contemplation: A Retreat at the Abbey of Gethsemani*, ed. Jane Marie Richardson (New York: Farrar, Straus and Giroux, 1992), 194–95.
7. Ibid., 57.

Sabbath Sentiments V: A Palace in Time; Not a Date but an Atmosphere

Abraham Joshua Heschel reminds us that "on the Sabbath we especially care for the seed of eternity planted in the soul." He notes that the "world has our hands, but our Soul belongs to Someone Else." The Sabbath "is not an interlude but the climax of living." He asserts, "Even thinking of business or labor should be avoided. Labor is a craft, but perfect rest is an art. It is the result of an accord of body, mind and imagination." So the seventh day "is a *palace in time* which we build. It is made of soul, of joy and reticence." Then "the love of the Sabbath is the love of man for what he and God have in common." Further, "the seventh day is like a palace in time with a kingdom for all. It is not a date but an atmosphere."[1]

On the Sabbath, "we learn the art of *surpassing* civilization." We are to spend the Sabbath in charm, grace, peace, and great love. Rabbi Heschel cites Exodus 35:3, "Ye shall kindle no fire throughout your habitations on the Sabbath day," and suggests that it is a "double sin to show anger on the Sabbath," for the ancient rabbis interpreted the Exodus exhortation to mean that "one must kindle no fire—not even the fire of righteous indignation."[2]

On the Sabbath, we "reclaim our authentic state, in which we may partake of a blessedness in which we are what we are, regardless of whether we are learned or not, of whether our career is a success or failure; it is a day of independence of social conditions." Heschel declares, "It is a sin to be sad on the Sabbath."[3]

The Sabbath path, then, is an invitation to travel in gratitude the road to holiness through wholeness for those called to be people of peace, immersed in God's reign, striving at the invitation of Jesus to be perfected as the heavenly Father is perfect (Matt 5:48). To decide that this is our posture is to live in such a way as to demonstrate that in the Sabbath lies our hope. We do not need more.

Notes

1. Abraham Joshua Heschel, *The Sabbath* (New York: Farrar, Straus and Giroux, 1951), 13, 14, 15, 16, 21.
2. Ibid., 27, 29.
3. Ibid., 30, 31.

Saints among Saints

In celebrating and living the mysteries, we become extraordinary. The call to prayer before the tenth solemn intercession on Good Friday suggests that we ask God to "cleanse the world of all errors, / banish disease, drive out hunger, / unlock prisons, loosen fetters, / granting to travelers safety, to pilgrims return, / health to the sick, and salvation to the dying." All of this is the business of the reign of God, the church's holy agenda, to which we annually pledge ourselves when we renew our baptismal promises by which we "promised to serve God in the holy Catholic Church" (See 55, Easter Vigil, *Roman Missal*).

The tasks and duties of the church belong to all of us. John Paul II notes,

> The sharing of all the baptized in the one priesthood of Jesus Christ is the key to understanding the Council's call for full, conscious and active participation in the liturgy (*Sacrosanctum Concilium*, 14). Full participation certainly means that every member of the community has a part to play in the liturgy; and in this respect a great deal has been achieved in parishes and communities across your land. But full participation does not mean that everyone does everything, since this would lead to a clericalizing of the laity and a laicizing of the priesthood; and this was not what the Council had in mind. The liturgy, like the Church, is intended to be hierarchical and polyphonic, respecting the different roles assigned by Christ and allowing all the different voices to blend in one great hymn of praise.[1]

Respecting our different roles will certainly suggest not just that each has a role to play, but that each is obliged to play that role consciously and actively.

Note

1. John Paul II, address to the bishops of the Episcopal conference of the United States, *Ad Limina* visit (October 9, 1998), 3.

Save a Soul by Picking Up a Needle

Saint Thérèse of Lisieux is said to have stated, "You can save a soul by picking up a needle." Even our smallest acts are significant. In fact, there are no neutral acts or thoughts, it seems to me. Anything we say or do, or omit saying or doing, either brings us closer to the fullness of God's reign or delays that fulfillment.

The *Catechism of the Catholic Church* teaches, "*The charity of Christ is the source in us of all our merits* before God. Grace, by uniting us to Christ in active love, ensures the supernatural quality of our acts and consequently their merit before God and before men. The saints have always had a lively awareness that their merits were pure grace" (CCC 2011). And Saint Thérèse is then and there quoted:

"After earth's exile, I hope to go and enjoy you in the fatherland, but I do not want to lay up merits for heaven. I want to work for your *love alone*. . . . In the evening of this life, I shall appear before you with empty hands, for I do not ask you, Lord, to count my works. All our justice is blemished in your eyes. I wish, then, to be clothed in your own *justice* and to receive from your *love* the eternal possession of *yourself* [St. Thérèse of Lisieux, "Act of Offering," in *Story of a Soul*, tr. John Clarke (Washington, DC: ICS, 1981), 277]" (2011).

Clothed in God's justice; beginning with that needle, perhaps!

SBNR

Jesus promises, "if I go and prepare a place for you, I will come back again and take you to myself, so that where I am you also may be." He adds, "Where [I] am going you know the way." Thomas is the perfect straight man: "Master, we do not know where you are going; how can we know the way?" And Jesus replies, "I am the way and the truth and the life" (John 14:3-6).

The many in our own age who are fond of telling us, "I am SBNR (spiritual but not religious)" may think that Jesus is reading from their playbook here or singing from their hymnal in inviting them to follow him. We might be tempted to reduce his whole invitation to a simple philosophy: "Jesus was nice. So I should be nice too." Neither of these approaches represents the church's philosophy or practice. Clearly, for the faithful, our religion and our spirituality are of the same fabric. And nice is not good enough.

Jesus, in part 1 of his farewell discourse in John's gospel, speaks of himself as the Way, a term later used by the earliest Christians to describe the Jesus movement, the church. The Way, then, is not a solitary path, nor a private thoroughfare on which my individual spirituality guides me until I come to the reward prepared for me in a distant time and place. In short, it is not all about me. Instead, it is a corporate enterprise. We come together as the Body of Christ; individually, we are members of that Body. I am never alone on the Jesus Way. In fact, in presenting a vision of the idealized church, the book of Acts lets us know that our spirituality is not a private matter or a solitary path. Rather, the Way runs through and includes the human community, even and especially those we might not first choose to include. In fact, Acts shows the early version of what has come to be called the fundamental option for the poor in which we care first for those who are oppressed, marginalized, or impoverished in any way. We care first for the distressed because Jesus cared first for them. We who seek to follow the Way must do as he has done.

Notice the complaint in Acts about the "widows [who] were being neglected in the daily distribution." The leadership heard the complaint, called the community together, proposed a solution, and the "proposal was acceptable to the whole community." How remarkable is that? And the "word of God continued to spread, and the number of the disciples in Jerusalem increased greatly" (6:1, 5, 7). Thus was born the church's diaconal ministry, the ministry of sustainable change for the most vulnerable people of the world. This ministry is shared by all the church and every member of the Body of Christ. We should note that seven were chosen in the report from Acts. This is not merely a historical note. As seven is symbolically regarded as the perfect number, we must see ourselves as among those in every age and place who are called and filled with God's good spirit.

When we are sprinkled with holy water on the Sundays of Easter, we are to remember our baptismal dignity as daughters and sons of the most high God, sisters and brothers together in the Body that is the church. We are to remember as well our promise to serve God faithfully in the church. This service entails both prayer and good works.

With our lives shaped by this insight, and bound together as we follow the Way, we pray confidently as the psalmist instructs us: "May your mercy, Lord, be upon us; as we put our hope in you" (33:22). For we are, as Peter's first letter affirms, "living stones . . . built into a spiritual house." We who have emerged, radiant, from the baptismal pool are called from darkness to light, "a chosen race, a royal priesthood, a holy nation, a people of his own" (2:5, 9). We hear and follow the Way, the One who calls out, "Do not let your hearts be troubled" (John 14:1).

Sensus Fidelium

> Since it was the will of God's only-begotten Son
> that [wo]men should share in his divinity,
> he assumed our nature in order that by becoming man
> he might make [wo]men gods.
>
> — Thomas Aquinas, *Opusc.* 57: 1–4, cited in *Catechism of the Catholic Church*, 460.

I was out in Burlington, Vermont, when their annual Jazz Fest was underway. Together with Fr. Brian Cummings, SSE, director of Edmundite Campus Ministry at Saint Michael's College in Burlington, I went downtown to hear Jerome Monachino and company play in their ensemble, Eight 02. Walking down Church Street, we saw a group of six to eight uncommonly tall, willowy young men who turned out to be members of the University of Vermont basketball team. Standing among them, looking up, Brian asked a question they had perhaps heard previously, "Do you guys play basketball?" The tallest of them, looking down at the tops of our heads, asked wryly in return, "How did you know?"

Some things, it turns out, are just obvious. The fact that God's people should participate fully and actively in the church's life and liturgy is chief among these things. The sense of the faithful is that we are sharers in the mystery and in the mission. We know this truth deep in our hearts. At our baptism, and when we annually renew our baptismal promises, we pledge to serve God faithfully in the church. We fulfill that promise by full and active participation.

What we know almost intuitively is, I think, what the church calls the *sensus fidei*: "a supernatural appreciation of the faith (*Sensus fidei*) shown by the universal consent in matters of faith and morals manifested by the whole body of the faithful under the guidance of the Magisterium" (*Catechism of the Catholic Church* glossary).

Because dignity and value are the properties of all the members of the faithful, the laity no less than the cardinals, the earliest church fathers understood that truth is either sensed or recognized by all the faithful—from the pope to the last one to arrive for Mass. Thus all participate, according to our different roles, in the great polyphony. Augustine observed that this understanding reaches to all: *ab episcopis usque ad extremos laicos fidelis* (from the bishops to the last of the faithful laity). Consequently, the Dogmatic Constitution on the Church (*Lumen Gentium*) of Vatican II, speaking of the *sensus fidelium* in section 12, did not so much make a decree as recognize and assert a reality:

> The holy people of God shares also in Christ's prophetic office: it spreads abroad a living witness to him, especially by a life of faith and love and by offering to God a sacrifice of praise, the fruit of lips confessing his name (see Heb 13:15). The whole body of the faithful who have received an anointing which comes from the holy one (see 1 Jn 2:20 and 27) cannot be mistaken in belief. It shows this characteristic faith, when, "from the bishops to the last of the faithful," it manifests a universal consensus in matters of faith and morals. By this sense of the faith, aroused and sustained by the Spirit of truth, the people of God, guided by the sacred magisterium which it faithfully obeys, receives not the word of human beings, but truly the word of God (see 1 Th 2:13).

So, after the Jazz Fest and in the shadow of those towering young basketball players who reminded us that some things are and ought to be obvious, Fr. Brian and I talked all these things over with his extraordinary staff of campus ministers, who are the very embodiment of a truly collaborative church. In fact, the Edmundite Campus Ministry team at Saint Michael's is the best funded, well-equipped, capable, and inspirationally staffed group of campus ministers I have met anywhere in my travels. They and their efforts are a localized example of what true collaboration in a spirit of discipleship looks like. Whenever I have been with them, I have heard the voice of Jesus, "Go and do likewise."

They wisely observed that in celebrating and living the mysteries, we become extraordinary. Just as the ordinary bread and wine go beyond their ordinary meaning and become for us the Body and Blood of Christ, so also do our ordinary lives go beyond what first we thought they might mean or signify and show us the rich and transforming presence of Christ who, by humbling himself to share in our humanity, promises us a share in his divinity.

When we know these things, we continue day by day to cultivate sanctity as Benedict advises in his Rule for monasteries, that the prayer of our lips might sanctify and fructify all our labors. This is the universal call to holiness. Hearing that call, living out our different roles, our primary act of evangelism is in giving the witness of holy lives. This transformative witness of each member of the Body is, in fact, what the business majors among us might call good marketing: those with whom we live and move and have our being should be helped to see the mystical reality that attracts us as moths to flame, so that all can readily observe how Christians love one another.

Baptism enfolds and incorporates us; the Spirit differentiates our roles within the discipleship. And "we hold this treasure in earthen vessels, that the surpassing power may be of God and not from us" (2 Cor 4:7). On pilgrimage, we hear the voice of God: "My grace is sufficient for you, for power is made perfect in weakness" (2 Cor 12:9). We who are sacramental people, we who are the pilgrim church, are on the road with Jesus. We are called to spend a lifetime exclaiming to each other, "Were not our hearts burning [within us] while he spoke to us on the way and opened the scriptures to us?" We too must "set out at once" to carry this message, fully, consciously, and actively participating in the mystery (Luke 24:32-33).

Serendipitous Wisdom

Perhaps I am slower than most in putting together all the pieces of what life in Christ might be for us, and how it challenges us in preparing to greet the fullness of God's reign. So I've been at work rethinking things, paying particular attention to the serendipitous and sometimes accidental wisdom of a number of my students.

When Dr. Martin Marty, the acclaimed church historian, visited our campus at my invitation a while back, I sent a number of students to hear him. One young scholar wrote a report afterwards in which he observed, "I noticed that many people were laughing as Dr. Marty spoke and sometimes nodding in agreement. I did not know what was funny or what they might be agreeing with. And this put me into a bit of a funk for about 30 minutes until I realized that this is why I have come to college: eventually I will know why the others are nodding and laughing. If I keep doing what I am supposed to be doing, in four years, I will be laughing, too."

Listening to this story in a different class, Ruth, another student, interjected, "Will you tell us again what Saint Augustine said when he called people to the eucharistic table, and isn't this kind of what is going on with this young guy?" Yes, I will and yes, it is: "Behold what you are; become what you receive." We are the Body of Christ; we seek to become more perfectly that which we already are: the Body of Christ. We continue to pray, "may we come to share in the divinity of Christ / who humbled himself to share in our humanity" (Liturgy of the Eucharist).

That young man, a music major and football player, is busy getting a truly liberal education in the Catholic intellectual tradition, which is a good thing for a young Methodist to have. As he seeks both to understand and to laugh, he reveals himself to be about 173 pounds of what St. Benedict described in his Rule for monasteries: "the Lord often reveals what is better to the younger" (3.3). I see the truth in his observation more clearly with every passing semester. But what Benedict does not say is equally to be noted, I think. For example, when he calls for "unhesitating obedience," he intends that "they carry out the superior's order as promptly as if the command came from God himself" (5.1, 4). Note that he does not say that the superior is always correct, only that the monastic is to obey with alacrity. Likewise in the matter of listening to all. While "all should be called for counsel," and all should be heard, including the young, not every utterance will be wise or holy (3.3).

Listening to the young does not mean that all they speak is wisdom. I asked one day in a class of eager college frosh who had recently completed papers analyzing the baptismal ritual, "How does one enter the church?" Their study might have prompted them to say, "One enters the church in the saving waters of baptism." That's what I thought. But not young James. "Well, you'd come in through the door, wouldn't you?" he asked. Umm, well, one might. I guess that's one approach.

Single or Celibate?

Being single may or may not be a temporary state in life. Those who hope that it will be temporary are involved in a dating scene in a way that seminarians and young priests are not. Celibacy offers a freedom that a single person in search of a mate does not have. Because we celibates do not seek mates, we need not engage in the rituals and worry that are part of the life, trials, and joys of those who do seek partners.

Some folks suggest, however, that we all begin life as celibate. Not true. We begin life single, or unmarried, but that is different from being celibate. Other folks incorrectly use the term celibacy to speak of a temporary abstinence from sexual activity. But, really, temporarily foregoing fornicating is not to claim a life of celibacy.

In seeking to explain celibacy, some will suggest that priests are married to the church. Well, that would not be very celibate of us, would it? Perhaps that kind of confusion relates to the practices and theologies of women religious, nuns and sisters, who have traditionally employed bridal imagery to speak of the relationship that they have with Christ in their vowed lives. These women religious wear rings to symbolize the image of the virginal bride of Christ. In fact, before the Second Vatican Council, a number of communities of religious women would have new members wear wedding gowns and veils on the day that they professed their vows, changing later into their religious habits. Male religious, priests and brothers, do not employ this wedding imagery to describe or define their own relationship to Christ or the church. Priests are not married to the church.

Pope Leo IX held a synod in 1049 that imposed celibacy on all clergy. That decree seems to have come about at least as much to safeguard church property from being handed on to the clerics' heirs as it was to promote spiritual concerns. Today, we know how celibacy was imposed; we know that the law could be changed; we understand that the discipline is really not essential to priesthood; we see any number of holy men, both married Orthodox priests and married former Anglicans, who have swum the Tiber to Rome where they have been reordained as priests; we see the estimable example of married Protestant clergy. So, we Romans sometimes seem, then, rather expected to view celibacy as anachronistic or outdated or unnecessary.

But celibacy remains the law of the church for priests and for deacons whose wives die. Singleness is a different state, though it may be temporary or permanent, chosen freely, or dictated by circumstance. These are differences in states of life, not necessarily better or worse, but different. Recognizing and appreciating diversity is key as we seek the fullness of God's reign.

Sirens, Whistles, and the Reign of God

Back in the day when I lived in Chicago, I was invited one night to a party in the Lincoln Park neighborhood. Once there, I discovered that most of the partygoers, trendy, urban professionals, were about my age and, like me, had been raised up in Catholic grammar and high schools, and in Catholic colleges. When they learned that I was a priest, a good number of them made sure to tell me that they had thrown off the yoke of Catholicism, and now found bagels and cream cheese a more sophisticated source of nourishment on Sunday mornings than eucharistic bread. Here was one of my first clues that something was seriously amiss: I had recently moved from New York City to Chicago; I knew that there are no real bagels in Chicago; they are on the wrong side of the Hudson River, and the water is all wrong.

At some point during our cocktail chatter, a siren careened by, and one of the partygoers, a Chicago native, asked, "Remember when we were in grade school, and Sister would make us stop, be silent, and pray at the sound of a siren?" And they all laughed heartily. Their laugher was not in fond remembrance, but sounded derisive and mean-spirited. "Why is that funny?" I asked in all seriousness. No one answered; our conversation ended awkwardly, and we all drifted away to chat with others.

I am one of the Catholic school graduates who remains grateful for and continues to observe silence in the wake of sirens. When the fire whistle would blow from the Proctor Village Hall, or if a Wilcol Ambulance should scream by, Sister would put down her book, and we would place our pencils in their trays. She would instruct us to pray silently for all of those in distress. When the silent prayer ended, we may have prayed together an Our Father, a Hail Mary, and a Glory Be.

That was certainly a pious custom, but it did not then nor does it now seem at all humorous to me. Sister taught us that the world was bigger than we were, bigger than our classroom and bigger even than Saint Rose of Lima Parish. She knew who we were, and invited us to become better versions of ourselves, to stretch our hearts by being aware of and open to the needs of others. The sound of an alarm was to remind us of our shared humanity and our common concerns. Some of us, affected by her concern, continue to pray daily at the conclusion of our table grace, "And make us always mindful of the needs of others." Even the unchurched, alienated Catholics, and all people of goodwill should be able to say "Amen!" to that. Our prayer helped us then, as it does now, to shape our hearts more like the heart of Jesus: compassionate to all who suffer, even those we do not know by face or name. In this way, Sister invited us into a larger community, into a global vision, into the communion of the saints. Her concern was about the reign of God, and our place within that kingdom.

I am not sure how much time Sister spent in those halcyon days reading the sermons of St. Maximus of Turin, who wrote and preached in the late fourth and early fifth centuries. In an Epiphany sermon, he noted that "Christ is baptized, not to be made holy by the water, but to make the water holy"[1] Sister knew that she and we had been baptized in that same saving water that flows from the side of Christ, the same water for which the deer longs in Psalm 42. Because Christ is holy, the water is holy; and we who come up out of that water are holy as well. She called us to recognize that we were members of the Body of Christ, and invited us to seek to come to full stature as boys and girls, one day to be men and women, every day and every moment members of that Body.

Saint Maximus noted that the pillar of fire went before the sons and daughters of Israel through the Red Sea so they could follow on their brave journey. At the time of the exodus, the pillar provided light for the people to follow; now, it gives light to the hearts of believers. "Then it made a firm pathway through the waters; now it strengthens the footsteps of faith in the bath of baptism."[2]

Sister knew all of that in her heart and in her bones. She invited us into that mystery, helping us participate in a reality beyond us, but encompassing us, calling us to wholeness and to holiness. May she, and all who labored with and like her, come to the fullness of God's glory, along that sure pathway that is the heart of Jesus.

Notes

1. Saint Maximus of Turin, Sermon 100, qtd. in *The Liturgy of the Hours*, vol. 1 (New York: Catholic Book Publishing, 1975), 612–13.
2. Ibid.

Some Solstice Thoughts for Winter

We Christian people rarely read in our liturgies from the Old Testament book titled the Song of Songs, attributed to that great king and lover, Solomon. In fact, it is the few books of the Bible not assigned for reading to the eucharistic assembly on Sundays. Perhaps this is because it is the only book of the Bible that does not mention God (at least by name). Or maybe that it is a bit racy in the imagery it uses in describing love, the lover, and the beloved. (Making this observation in a college classroom is a sure way to ensure that college students will spend some time in *lectio divina* [or *lectio curiositas*] that same day.)

But on December 21, we are given an option of reading at Mass either from the Song of Songs (2:8-14) or from the book of the prophet Zephaniah (3:14-18a). Choosing to proclaim the pericope from the Song of Songs is a great solstice choice. In it, we read of the lover: "The sound of my lover! here he comes / springing across the mountains, / leaping across the hills." This lover peers "through the lattices." Sneaky, or head-over-tea-cup in love? Then: "My lover speaks." We wait! "and says to me, / 'Arise, my friend, my beautiful one, / and come!'"

Wait for it: "For see, the winter is past, / the rains are over and gone. / The flowers appear on the earth, / the time of pruning the vines has come, / and the song of the turtledove is heard in our land."

Winter is over? Not in Duluth; we had snow up to the navel of an average-sized person. But: the longest night and shortest day signal that the earth has turned and the journey to the sun begins again. We Christians claim these days for our feast of the Unconquerable Son, the mystery of whose humble birth we celebrate with festivity and due reverence. The feast rouses in us gratitude for those gifts yet to come.

Speaking of Doors: Shepherd, Gate, and Lamb

Jesus seems to be presented as a bit of a mixed metaphor, a profusion of images, in the Good Shepherd discourse in John's tenth chapter and in First Peter. Jesus is the sheep gate. As a good shepherd and not a hireling, he himself lies down across the opening of the sheepfold. A thief or marauder would have to step over his body to enter and have access to the sheep. Alert and courageous, laying down his very body, he promises and provides both hope and security.

But he is not just the gate: he is the shepherd whose voice the sheep recognize. They will not follow a stranger. And because he is the Good Shepherd, we have come to know "there is nothing I shall want." It is this One we seek, this One we must follow. To be in the church's communion is to be one with its founder and foundation, Jesus, the pioneer and perfecter of our faith. He is the gate through whom we must enter. He comes that we might have life, "and have it more abundantly." And we are left to ask what abundant life might look like.

We might come to understand the promise of abundant life by carefully considering the Scriptures. In First Peter, we are reminded that the resurrection is of a piece with the crucifixion just as the great three days are one liturgy. "By his wounds you have been healed," First Peter reminds us, and then repeats the image of the Suffering Servant we remember from Good Friday: "He committed no sin, / and no deceit was found in his mouth" (2:24, 22).

The profusion of images continues. Jesus, then, is not just the gate, not just the Shepherd, but also the Lamb of God, the new lamb by whose blood we have been redeemed. Unlike the first Passover lamb who was eaten and seen no more, this Lamb is alive always and everywhere, and continues to nourish and sustain the church in every age and place, from the rising of the sun to its setting. Paradoxically, he does not diminish but, rather, his Body, the church, grows and flourishes.

This new life of the Lamb of God is not one of isolation, but as members together in the sheepfold, each seeks transformation in the communion of the Holy Spirit whose breath calls us and binds us together as members of the Body of Christ. We encounter this shepherd at the twin tables of Word and Eucharist, in the communion of saints ever present around us, and in the strangers and the marginalized, of whom the book of Acts speaks, in our shared call to *diaconia*, the service of those who are poor or oppressed in any way. So here, in *diaconia*, is the way to wholeness, holiness, the abundance of life.

As the gate, Jesus keeps marauders out; but he is also the gate through which we can enter and be saved. As the Shepherd, he leads and guides. As the Lamb, he nourishes and sustains. Andrew Greeley points out what the Scriptures tell us first: "Catholicism is a verdant rainforest of metaphors."[1] A metaphor is a comparison that shows how two things that are not alike in most ways are similar in one important way. In metaphor, we meet the Lord. And in the Lord, we find the Way. Having met and seeking to follow the Way, we must continue to ask what was asked of Peter and the eleven in Acts, chapter 2: "What are we to do?" We are to continue to repent, for this is the work of a lifetime, seeking the transformation for which the deacon or priest prays silently on behalf of us all when water is added to the wine at the preparation of the gifts: "By the mystery of this water and wine / may we come to share in the divinity of Christ / who humbled himself to share in our humanity" (Liturgy of the Eucharist). There is our goal, and we await the promised Spirit of God who will lead us on, guiding us to verdant pastures and right paths.

Note

1. Andrew Greeley, *The Catholic Imagination* (Los Angeles: University of California Press, 2000), 9.

Stand Tall

I was singing with a men's chorus of faculty and students one day when Dr. Bret, our conductor, looked up and commanded briskly, "Gentlemen, stand tall!" The student next to me, a lanky, boy-faced kid who was about six foot four, looked down at the fellow standing next to him who was a foot shorter. With a look of amused condescension, he said to him, "Do your best."

Short guys are not amused by that kind of humor; one smaller guy made reference later to "taking a jab at the short kids." Such was not Dr. Bret's intention, it seems to me. His real direction was to ask us to come to our full stature, stretching beyond what seemed at first comfortable or even possible. It was not an invitation to compare ourselves to the lanky, to wish to be someone other than we are. Perhaps the intent is better expressed in one of the prayers from the 1998 translation of *The Roman Missal* that did not get final approval for our use. On the Eleventh Sunday in Ordinary Time, we (would have) asked God, "at whose bidding the seed will sprout / and the shoot grow toward full stature" to hear our prayers, helping us to "trust in your hidden ways, / that we may pray with confidence / and wait for your kingdom / now growing in our midst."

Maybe, then, Joey wasn't so much taking a jab as offering advice; we should indeed do our best, each according to his ability and gifts. There, in fact, is the key: confidence in God's unfolding plan. We stand tall in anticipation, both tall Joey and the kid next to him: reaching for the stars as the apostle Paul suggested, "until we all attain to the unity of faith and knowledge of the Son of God, to mature manhood, to the extent of the full stature of Christ" (Eph 4:13).

Summer Peace

[The rich man] said, "This is what I shall do: I shall tear down my barns and build larger ones. There I shall store all my grain and other goods and I shall say to myself, 'Now as for you, you have so many good things stored up for many years, rest, eat, drink, be merry!'" But God said to him, "You fool, this night your life will be demanded of you; and the things you have prepared, to whom will they belong?" Thus will it be for the one who stores up treasure for himself but is not rich in what matters to God.

— Luke 12:18-21

On a recent August Saturday, before heading off to the parish where I share weekend duties, I went off for a morning swim. Before jumping in, I stood in the northern Minnesota lake in cool water up to my waist. There were no clouds in the sky, no boats or jet skis on the lake, not another swimmer in sight, nor anyone visible on shore. A very certain peace enfolded me, and the concerns and anxieties of the day slipped away. The homily not yet ready for prime time, the urgency of grocery shopping for dinner, the prospect of the impending return to the classroom rushing at me like a runaway train: all of these faded away in the presence of grace.

In a flash, and without thinking about it, I understood the mystical Julian of Norwich's comforting promise: "All is well, and all is well, and all will ever be well." I felt a deep and abiding sense of gratitude and a call to make thanksgiving, and knew that I was rich in the things that matter to God. And just then I resolved to delay indefinitely all plans to build a bigger barn.

Sweet Mystery of Life

In 1935, Jeanette Macdonald and Nelson Eddy starred in the MGM film *Naughty Marietta*, in which they made famous the song "Ah! Sweet Mystery of Life." You can hear and see them on YouTube. But Jesus announced the discovery long before that the mystery of life is found in the exercise of compassion. Paul reports the teaching and the example of Jesus: "be kind to one another, compassionate, forgiving one another as God has forgiven you in Christ." Paul then invites us to behave like God: "be imitators of God, as beloved children, and live in love." He reminds us, "For you were once darkness, but now you are light in the Lord." We must then "Live as children of light" (Eph 4:32; 5:1-2, 8).

We see the compassion of Jesus at work in Luke's report: Jesus "was teaching in a synagogue on the sabbath. And a woman was there who for eighteen years . . . was bent over, completely incapable of standing erect. When Jesus saw her, he called to her and said, 'Woman, you are set free of your infirmity'" (Luke 13:10-12; see 13:13-17). Just as we are certain that he will heal us of our own infirmities, so should we seek to imitate him in the compassion we show to all those we meet. Then we too will have found, ah!, the sweet mystery of life.

That Mourning Beatitude

> Blessed are they who mourn,
> for they will be comforted.
>
> — Matthew 5:4

The Beatitudes give us images of the reign of God both present in our own day and awaiting fulfillment in heaven. When we attend to Jesus with the ear of our hearts, when we attune our hearts to the voice of the shepherd and invite him to teach us, we shape ourselves, our families, our parishes, and our world according to the Word. Sometimes we see hearts conformed to the heart of Jesus, and then we know that we are not far from the reign of God.

All of us who seek transformation in Christ do well to be aware of the presence of grace and to know with full confidence that "It is good to have our hearts strengthened by grace" (Heb 13:9). That enduring lesson for us is celebrated in George Bernanos's delightful novel, *The Diary of a Country Priest*. In it, the priest wisely observes, "Grace is everywhere."

Even mourning can be a grace, bring grace, or invite grace. The particular grace of the mourning church gathered at prayer finds us confident and unafraid, though still we mourn. Jesus speaks to us who mourn, promising, "Blessed are they who mourn, for they will be comforted." Our shared faith tells us that we will meet again in the place where every tear will be wiped away. In that new world where the fullness of God's peace will be revealed, people of every race, language, and way of life will be gathered to share in the one eternal banquet.

So we pray that we will know the reality experienced and described by Hildegard of Bingen in the twelfth century: "God hugs you. You are encircled by the arms of the mystery of God."

May we continue to come to the Eucharist to be strengthened with food for the journey, giving us peace and consolation. May it cleanse us, forgive our sins, and bring us, in the company of the saints and angels, rejoicing before the face of God.

There Is No Winter in the Church's Year

> [M]ay no earthly undertaking hinder those
> who set out in haste to meet your Son,
> but may our learning of heavenly wisdom
> gain us admittance to his company.
> — Collect for the Second Sunday of
> Advent

All of our Christian life is characterized by waiting. Day by day, we wait for the second coming: Jesus, once born among us, will come again in glory as the Just Judge. Our intent and our prayerful hope is that when he comes, he will find us watching in prayer, engaged in good works, our hearts filled with wonder and praise. This is our concern in every season of the church year and each day of our lives. As we consider the risks necessary to shape our world according to the call of God's good Spirit, we can seek out every opportunity to rekindle in our own souls and hearts the power of God's presence and, in turn, to make that truth apparent to others by thoughtful prayer and active concern.

The joy we anticipate should be the model for the joy we seek to cultivate day by day. We have a model for such aesthetic behavior in Dorothy Day. In her book *On Pilgrimage*, the Catholic Worker cofounder advises that we must cultivate divine life. She points to the Scripture verse, "Whether you eat or whether you drink, do all for the glory of God [1 Cor 10:31]." She concludes, "This does not mean that we do not enjoy our spaghetti for lunch. God gives us natural happiness too, in order to help us love him."[1] We who live in the embrace of the communion of saints ought to understand and seek out that natural happiness. We are called to make our every thought, word, and deed opportunities to embrace goodness. Surely this idea is a model for how we should view our daily lives, and a guide for us in seeking the reign of God.

In the collect for the Second Sunday of Advent, we ask that "no earthly undertaking hinder those / who set out in haste to meet your

Son, / but may our learning of heavenly wisdom / gain us admittance to his company." This suggests that, in every season, the landscape of the human heart be cultivated in such a way that Christ will find a welcome.

Peter's epistle reminds us, "But the day of the Lord will come like a thief." As we wait, he asks, "what sort of persons ought [you] to be," and quickly suggests "conducting yourselves in holiness and devotion, waiting for and hastening the coming of the day of God." He advises, "be eager to be found without spot or blemish before him, at peace" (2 Pet 3:10, 11-12, 14).

As the weeks of Ordinary Time roll on, as spring turns to summer, we remember, as the Benedictine liturgical scholar Odo Casel wrote years ago, "There is no winter in the church's year; if it starts up again, circle forming on circle, this constant return is to suggest the divine quality of the mystery. St. Ambrose in one of his morning hymns calls Christ, 'the true day which shines on day, the true Sun which casts everlasting splendour.' Christ is therefore 'the day which is splendid with the light that knows no evening.'"[2]

Light-filled days are our opportunity to rekindle the power of God's presence. We wait in joyful hope until God's plan is perfectly fulfilled, praying, as we have in the second eucharistic prayer for reconciliation, that in the new world where the fullness of God's peace will be revealed, people of every race, language, and way of life may be gathered to share in the one eternal banquet with Jesus Christ the Lord.

Notes

1. Dorothy Day, *On Pilgrimage* (Grand Rapids: Eerdmans, 1999), 193.
2. Odo Casel, "The Church's Year," in *The Mystery of Christian Worship* (London: Darton, Longman & Todd, 1962), quoted in *The Glenstal Book of Readings for the Seasons*, 18 (Collegeville, MN: Liturgical Press, 2008).

"The One Who Blasphemes against the Holy Spirit Will Not Be Forgiven"

When we hear Jesus pronounce, "the one who blasphemes against the holy Spirit will not be forgiven" (Luke 12:10), we find it very unsettling. But attempting to determine what it means to blaspheme against the Holy Spirit is not so easy. Poking around in different study sites and biblical resources, we get the idea that this kind of blasphemy might include asserting that liberation comes from Satan's power rather than the indwelling Holy Spirit. This would be a kind of continued unbelief. If, throughout our lives and at the moment of death, we reject the gifts of the Holy Spirit prompting us to trust in Jesus, that could be unpardonable blasphemy. This would mean that we consistently and deliberately reject God's mercy and ascribe the Spirit's work to the devil.

Let us be clear: this is an extraordinary sin, and we probably have not met such a sinner. It is beyond unlikely that your average congregant could sin in that way. It is certainly not a sin we could accidentally commit, even on a very bad day. We must hear Jesus not threatening us, but speaking words of great comfort and promise: "everyone who acknowledges me before others the Son of Man will acknowledge before the angels of God" (12:8). We remember and give thanks that the apostle Paul prays for all of us in every age and place: "May the eyes of [your] hearts be enlightened" (Eph 1:18).

Tragedy and the Will of God

On a fine Wednesday in July 2003, I was moving some items on a bookshelf and came across a framed pencil-and-crayon portrait of me, done in May 1989, signed by its artist, "Sam Cox, Age 7." Sam had added a note on the left side of the picture, "I like you Fr. Graham." Well, I liked Sam a lot too. It is quite a child, one with a nicely developed sense of self, who would be confident that the adults in his life would love to have a piece of his art and would want it framed too, so that it could be cherished forever.

Sam had an astonishing sense of awe and wonder. He was so enthused about so much that, in telling the tales of the things that intrigued him, he would often gasp for air as the words flew. Sam's personality was a gift of God wisely and gently nurtured by an exceptional mom and dad. I had not seen Sam for a number of years, but felt confident that he had grown into a fine young man. I gave thanks briefly for his gifts, and returned the portrait to its place on the shelf.

Evening came and morning followed. Thursday, walking back from the mailbox with the morning paper, I was saddened to read the banner headline on page 1 of the *Duluth News Tribune*: "Crash Kills ex-Duluthian," but stunned to read the subhead: "Marshall School graduate Sam Cox dies when his Navy helicopter crashes in Italy." Then followed a classic piece of denial: it could not be the same Sam Cox; it must be someone else. But details confirmed that it was he: the names of the parents, and of the siblings, and that he was a graduate of St. Michael's School where we first met when I had been his pastor. Sam had died at just about the time I had been admiring his 1989 gift of art.

Later, I felt an unsettling sense of anger. Many of the university students I encounter have little sense of awe and wonder, often no passion, or particular interest in much of anything. Too many seem to seek to hustle through college so they can get a job, raise a family, retire, and die. And here is a young man passionate about life and opportunity, dead at age twenty-one in a fiery crash near Sicily with three other crew members. "Helicopters, they're kind of dangerous," his father said. But he also reported that Sam "read *The Hunt for Red October* in fifth grade and after that it was all Navy."

Sam had been in Iraq, and sent a friend an e-mail in April in which he wrote, "I have dropped off tons of food supplies in cities and I have seen what needs to be done." Conscious of the great division about the justice or wisdom of the war in Iraq, on the Sixteenth Sunday in Ordinary Time, thinking of Sam's good efforts and noble intent, I prayed with cracking voice and misted eyes that God "Keep us alive in Christ Jesus. Keep us watchful in prayer and true to his teaching till your glory is revealed in us."

One of his young friends remarked that Sam had died doing what he loved. We would all have preferred seeing him live to do what he loved. He played the tuba in the high school band, and electric bass and trombone with their jazz band. He was a Boy Scout and an altar server, an honors student in German, lettered in three sports, qualified first in his class as an aviation electronics mate and earned his Air Crew wings. He was to have entered the University of Missouri in January on a Seaman-to-Admiral scholarship to study electrical engineering and earn his commission as a Navy officer. He wanted to be a pilot.

Why did he die? Why are his parents left bereft, siblings shattered, extended family, friends, teachers, and pastors undone in grief? Why does the just one suffer? Even before the days of Job, humankind has asked these questions. We get the same response that Job got. If we persist in asking these questions in hope of a more detailed explanation from God, we can expect to be met by silence, which will be followed by anger, tailed by depression, leading to despair.

Our human response to tragedy is to seek to console ourselves, to make sense out of what is senseless. Not so long after Sam's death, four teenagers crashed in a car near the university where I taught. Two died and two were seriously injured. The next day, a student explained to me that it was God's will. Nonsense. God does not will tragedy, sorrow, loss, and pain. Our own experience and our Scriptures and the church's life of prayer make it evident that God does not will such events. There are accidents caused by nature, mechanical malfunction, inattention or carelessness. And someone driving carelessly who kills or injures others can hardly be seen as God's agent acting out the divine will. When we mistakenly assert that tragedy is God's will, it is usually a kind but misguided effort to speak comforting words in the face of unspeakable grief out of which we hope to weave a discernible plot. "Everything happens for a reason," these people might also assert. Well, no, some things just happen, and there is no reason or explanation. Such is the case in Sam's untimely death.

"Well, God just needed another angel," folks sometimes say as they hope to promote healing. But God, as the divine self is revealed to us, is not so hard up for angels that there is a need to strike down young people and give them wings.

Speaking with Sam's strong parents, Jo and Jody Cox, the day after his death, I had an excellent lesson in approaching death and loss. They did not ask the questions one might expect, did not wonder why their son had died and not another, did not rage at having enjoyed this beloved son for only 21 years and not 101. Instead, each of them remembered his smile, his goodness, his gentleness, his awe and wonder. "He is frozen in time for us," his dad said. "He's always going to be 21 with a fabulous smile."

Writing in *America* magazine two weeks before Sam's death, Sr. Dianne Bergant, CSA, noted that there are many people searching today, hungering for instruction, good people seeking direction. "They may be parents who are sick with grief over the future of a troubled child; a man stripped of his dignity by unemployment; a woman facing a pregnancy alone; elderly people who feel the diminishing surge of life in their bodies"; angry and confused people who have lost confidence in political or religious leaders. "They are people who are looking for answers and for meaning. They are like sheep without a shepherd. To whom should they turn?"[1]

Peter the apostle answers that question for us. Jesus, observing that many found his teachings hard and departed from him, asked the Twelve, "'Do you also want to leave?' Simon Peter answered him, 'Master, to whom shall we go? You have the words of eternal life'" (John 6:67-68).

I do not know why Sam died, but I do know why he lived. God's glory was revealed in Sam: we who were touched in and by his brief life have been schooled in the Spirit's gift of awe and wonder; we have experienced the transforming power of love; we have seen kindness at work and gentleness at play. The incarnate Christ lived in Sam, and Sam in him. We have glimpsed mystery, and God among us. In the face of this great gift, let us bless the Lord, and give Sam thanks!

I like you, Sam . . . a very great deal.

Note

1. Dianne Bergant, "To Whom Should We Turn?," *America* 189, no. 1 (July 7, 2003).

Transformation in Christ

Through the Spirit we acquire a likeness to God; indeed,
we attain what is beyond our most sublime aspirations—we
become God.

— St. Basil the Great, *On the Holy Spirit*[1]

Each celebration of the Eucharist invites us to consider our own role in the Body of Christ as baptized members. Participation in the eucharistic mystery amplifies the effects of baptism in cooperation with the Spirit of God for the renewal of both church and earth.

As we pilgrims progress, our temptation, in examining our consciences, is to begin to count: how many children taught, how many retreatants served or retreats made, how many people guided in spiritual direction, and how many temporal affairs of the church and parish attended to. Sometimes the sum seems staggering. And when we add our sum to the years of service of all our sisters and brothers, with those of all the parishioners buried in our cemeteries, the number moves beyond staggering to the border of unfathomable. But if we think life in Christ is only about service, we have missed the significant beginning on the day of baptism.

On our day of baptism, either we promised or our parents and godparents promised in our names that we would serve God faithfully in the Catholic Church. Those promises were received by the Lord through his church, present around the baptismal pool in the members of the gathered community. Hearing the voice of Jesus calling us to "repent and hear the good news," we each seek our own conversion, and that of all the world. Our task is to invite the Word of Christ to dwell richly within us (Col 4:16). What will this Word accomplish, working within us? Saint Athanasius tells us that "the Word of God 'was made [flesh] so that we might be made God.'"[2] Saint Thomas Aquinas points to the same truth: "The only-begotten Son of God, wanting to make us sharers in his divinity, assumed our nature, so that he, made man, might make [us] gods."[3]

This ancient insight is repeated at each Mass when the gifts are prepared. As the priest or deacon pours drops of water into the wine, he prays, "By the mystery of this water and wine / may we come to share in the divinity of Christ / who humbled himself to share in our humanity" (Liturgy of the Eucharist). Sometimes, however, we confuse the call to transformation with a simple vision of social justice. But immersion into the eucharistic mystery reveals the gospel insight that if we build a better earth, but do not become better people, if we do not glimpse the reign of God among us, then all of our accomplishments will be as straw and dust.

At the eucharistic table, we celebrate both transformation and faithfulness. The Eucharist calls us to an awareness that we must keep one eye on the past and another eye fixed on the future as we seek the "narrow gate" (Matt 7:14). Our hearts are directly connected to hands still wet with baptismal water. The apostle Paul speaks to these hearts and hands, reminding us that "the gifts and the call of God are irrevocable" (Rom 11:29). Calling us to lives of faithful prayer and constant service, our baptism into the Body of Christ speaks of our dignity and the glorious vocation we share: to show in our own lives the glory of God (see Isa 49:3). Catherine Mowry LaCugna writes of the message to us in the doctrine of the Trinity, affirming that the God into whose name we are baptized is not a patriarch who has created women less than men. Our God calls us to true communion among persons, and in the Spirit will share with us the deepest meaning of life.

Transformation in Christ will include openness to new situations and new needs. The Spirit will speak; we will listen, and the church will endlessly reform herself in every age and place, recovering, as LaCugna hopes, the earliest apostolic charisms and the message of the reign of God.[4]

The spirit-filled lives of those who have gathered before us at the eucharistic table and commune with us still inspire and enflame our hope. We read of them in the book of Revelation: "I heard a voice from heaven say, 'Write this: Blessed are the dead who die in the Lord from now on.' 'Yes,' said the Spirit, 'let them find rest from their labors, for their works accompany them'" (14:13). A new generation of those who think and pray keeps our hope in focus. The vigor and insight of these young scholars and the vitality they and their companions bring to the church today gives us confidence in asserting our own place, as Vatican II insists we must, among the people of God.

Our place in God's reign is envisioned and celebrated in William W. How's 1864 hymn that prompts us today to nod our thanks to those on our right, those on our left, and the saints who shine above: "O blest communion / family divine! / We feebly struggle, they in glory shine; / Yet all are one / within your great design" ("For All the Saints," verse 4).

Yes: "All of us, gazing with unveiled face on the glory of the Lord, are being transformed into the same image from glory to glory, as from the Lord who is the Spirit" (2 Cor 3:18).

And: Thanks be to God!

Notes

1. Qtd. in *The Liturgy of the Hours*, vol. 2 (New York: Catholic Book Publishing, 1975), 976.

2. Athanasius of Alexandria, *On the Incarnation of the Word*, 54, 3, qtd. in Pope Benedict XVI, *The Fathers of the Church: From St. Clement of Rome to St. Augustine of Hippo*, ed. Joseph T. Lienhard, 47 (Grand Rapids: Eerdmans, 2009).

3. Thomas Aquinas, *Opusc.* 57: 1–4, cited in *Catechism of the Catholic Church*, 2nd ed. (Libreria Editrice Vaticana, 1997), 460.

4. Catherine Mowry LaCugna, ed., "God in Communion with Us," in *Freeing Theology: The Essentials of Theology in Feminist Perspective* (New York: HarperCollins, 1993), 108.

The Tridentine Mass

I don't get this business with the Tridentine Mass. I should get it. I was in ninth grade at Cathedral High School when the first English translations were introduced. As a boy, I learned the Latin responses to the prayers at the foot of the altar and the other parts proper to the altar server. I could sing the proper parts of the Mass with our St. Rose of Lima School schola, as well as the ordinary parts, and could pronounce Latin far better than ever I understood it.

I have, but rarely, presided at the liturgy in Latin. A couple times, as a pastor, I worked to convince parishioners that we should celebrate at least one Mass on Pentecost Sunday in the *lingua antiqua* and sing the *Missa de Angelis*, Mass VIII. Afterwards, even daily-Mass Catholics would say, "Well that was a nice enough look at a museum piece, but I don't need to do that again." Still, I scheduled Mass in Latin, though the *Novus Ordo*, once recently for students at the college where I teach. They should know, or at least experience, that part of the tradition. That's what I told them, at least.

One of the most rigorously orthodox of our students said sweetly, succinctly, and accurately the morning after, "It was nice to be in touch with our tradition and to experience the Mass as did our grandparents, but there was a layer of meaning entirely absent." Her own experience was a far better teacher than any explanation I might have offered.

Catholic folks born in the 1950s often assert that they know Latin. Few do know it. Some will say, "I speak Latin." Or, "My mother speaks Latin." Then they greet me: "*Dominus vobiscum.*" I may be large, but I do not take the plural.

I recently attended a wedding of a delightful and delightfully traditional young couple who wanted part of their wedding liturgy sung in Latin. They did not recognize that the setting they employed for the *Sanctus* and *Agnus Dei* was from the *Requiem*. After mentioning this to another traditional young guest there, I was asked, "What, exactly, is a *Requiem*?"

Praying in Latin is not easy. Neither fond nostalgia for an era one never knew nor spending a couple semesters in Rome and ordering spaghetti carbonara in Italian gives one the ability to pronounce or understand the complexities of an ancient language one has never studied. One of my colleagues, a Latin professor, went one day to a local celebration of the Eucharist according to the extraordinary rite, the rite we usually refer to as Tridentine. Coming back to campus, shaking his head, the professor said sadly, "I don't know what that was, but it was not Latin."

So, what are the issues involved in restoring the Tridentine liturgy? Lisa Takeuchi Cullen wants "to experience the joy of communion without the anguish of our modern-day differences." She thinks she'll find that in the Tridentine Mass when the priest has his "back to the congregation and [is] speaking in a dead language." This, she thinks, will spare her homilies based on the priest's "Netflix queue." Good luck to her with all that.

Even back in the day, the homily or sermon was not in Latin. She could seek out a parish that celebrates the liturgy in a language unknown to her, Vietnamese, maybe, or Tagalog or Eritrean. She could then get what she seeks: "an hour-long meditation in the community of the faithful, reaffirming ancient beliefs in familiar but inscrutable chant." She opines, "I'm not so sure that isn't what the Apostles intended."[1] There is scant evidence to suggest that the apostles were big into inscrutability. Perhaps her opinion reveals a different desire: to decide herself what the apostles intended rather than trust the church in magisterial authority to interpret and mediate both Scripture and tradition with the wisdom of the ages.

The church, in the wisdom of the ages, prompts us to pray in languages we understand. Those who sentimentalize another reality should not seek to press it on others among the people of God.

The priests I know who intuit a pastoral need for the old rite did not grow up with it. Since the Mass in any language can and should be celebrated with reverence, the need for the old rite seems unclear. At least to me. Those who celebrate it cannot, on Monday morning, gather at the water cooler with other Catholics and a variety of other Christians and discuss the Scriptures they heard the day before; Trent's missal is different from today's Lectionary, with fewer Scripture pericopes and scant attention to the Old Testament.

When the Tridentine crowd prays on Good Friday for "the perfidious Jew," the rest of us know with certainty that God will hear what we ask, but we trust that he will give us what we truly need. This will surely not include perfidy, either among Catholics or Jews.

Together in the big tent that is the church, may we continue with faithfulness and good humor, and in all the languages of humankind, the church's unbroken tradition of coming "together to celebrate the paschal mystery . . . 'giving thanks to God for his inexpressible gift' (2 Cor 9:15) in Christ Jesus, 'in praise of his glory' (Eph 1:12) through the power of the Holy Spirit" (*Sacrosanctum Concilium* 6).

Note

1. Lisa Takeuchi Cullen, "I Confess, I Want Latin," *Time* (July 20, 2007): 60.

Trying Times

These are truly times that try our souls, but one thing becomes increasingly clear as the church continues to grow: Peter's insight will provoke and sustain us through all the ages. He heroically articulated his faith even as any number of other disciples abandoned Jesus, to the Lord's disappointment. Jesus fed the enormous crowd with bread from heaven. They were delighted by the free food. But when he addressed them with the bread of life discourse, many of the disciples said, "This is a hard saying; who can listen to it?" Their attraction to Jesus was based, it seems, on free food. When he suggested that the issue was bread of life and a new way of life, they were discouraged and went away. So, "Jesus then said to the Twelve, 'Do you also want to leave?'" Simon Peter answered him with heart-aching, graced-based loyalty, saying, "Master, to whom shall we go? You have the words of eternal life" (John 6:67-68). Here is the mantra for troubled or interesting times, the inspiration of faith to quicken us in hope: "You alone have the words of eternal life."

And what do we ask for our leaders? Consider the collect for the Mass for a council or synod in the Roman Missal: "O Lord, ruler and guardian of your Church, / pour out, we pray, upon your servants / a spirit of truth, understanding and peace, / that they may strive with all their heart / to know what is pleasing to you / and then pursue it with all their strength."

We do well to remember that about eleven years after the Lord's ascension, squabbles in the church were so threatening with "no little dissension and debate" that "Paul, Barnabas, and some of the others [were appointed to] go up to Jerusalem to the apostles and presbyters" (Acts 15:2). At question was the relationship of the incipient church to the synagogue. Did new converts to the faith first have to become Jews? Must one keep kosher and must males submit to circumcision in order to follow Jesus? "The apostles and the presbyters met together to see about this matter" (15:6). In announcing the decision, their letter reported, "It is the decision of the holy Spirit and of us . . . " (15:28).

And thus the nascent church begins to separate from the synagogue, a move more decisive and dramatic and with farther reaching consequence than any act a council could promulgate today. Those dismayed by division, disagreement, and unpleasantness in the church in our own day should remember this lesson from Acts. The German Baptist minister Walter Rauschenbusch, prophet of the American Social Gospel movement early in the last century, observed that the disciples could not keep pace with the sweep of the Master, fluttering where he soared. This is a truth that is observable in every age.

Historians tell us that fifty years of tumult follow every ecumenical council. We now know that the tumult will be extended in the wake of Vatican II, perhaps because global communications make the conversation and the squabbles more accessible to greater numbers of participants. Sometimes, it seems, those who appear to oppose any movement or modification or *aggiornamento* are the poor we will always have with us (see Matt 26:11 and Mark 14:7). When we are at odds, when we have visions that seem incompatible, we might be called to realize that God's reign in all its fullness is still in our future.

Visions of Radiance

One of the crankiest priests I've known was awakened in the wee hours of Christmas morning once by an inebriated caller who asked, "Do you know what time Masses are?" He answered, "Yes, I do." Then hung up unceremoniously: click. But the question most asked by December callers to rectories is, "What time is Midnight Mass?" The December 2012 calendar for the Cathedral of Christ the King in Superior, Wisconsin, notes, "Midnight Mass. Yep, midnight."

The 2011 translation of *The Roman Missal* seems to have anticipated that question by offering prayers "At the Mass during the Night" where the Sacramentary of Paul VI had offered "Mass at Midnight." The collect in the newer translation addresses the God who made this most sacred night radiant with the splendor of the true light. We pray that we who have known the mysteries of this light on earth may also delight in his gladness in heaven.

It makes very good sense, then, that our awe and gratitude inspire us to kneel at the Christmas feast when, in the Creed, we say the words, "and by the Holy Spirit was incarnate of the Virgin Mary, / and became man." Visions of radiance call for bended knees and grateful hearts.

Washing Feet

Note how specific this rubric is for Holy Thursday: "the washing of the feet follows the homily." For reasons that seem to contradict the gospel, some presiders invite people to wash their hands instead. Go figure. Jesus has already ruled on this practice in his reply to Peter in John's gospel proclaimed just moments before: "Simon Peter said to him, 'Master, then not only my feet, but my hands and head as well.' Jesus said to him, 'Whoever has bathed has no need except to have his feet washed'" (John 13:9-10).

Some congregations omit the ritual footwashing entirely. It is hard to give a reason to support their innovation given the response of Jesus to Peter, who had first wanted no part of the ritual: "Peter said to him, 'You will never wash my feet.' Jesus answered him, 'Unless I wash you, you will have no inheritance with me'" (John 13:8).

Note also the directive: "At the beginning of the Liturgy of the Eucharist, there may be a procession of the faithful in which gifts for the poor may be presented." Could there be a day better suited for such a procession with checks and cash, foodstuffs, clothing, and whatever else might be needed locally, nationally, or internationally? During the procession, it is suggested that "Where true charity is dwelling, God is present there" be sung. What hymn could be more appropriate?

Washing feet and submitting to having our feet washed is part of the Christian experience. The ritual expression on Holy Thursday reminds us of what our lives are to look like day by day.

We Are What We Repeatedly Do

Aristotle is reported to have written that we are what we repeatedly do. It turns out that while he may have thought and taught that, the sentence actually belongs to Will Durant. He did quote Aristotle in *The Story of Philosophy: The Lives and Opinions of the World's Greatest Philosophers*: "virtues are formed in man by his doing the actions." But Durant himself added, "we are what we repeatedly do."[1] He made the point that excellence is a habit rather than an act.

One could certainly argue, it seems to me, that

- if grace builds on nature, and
- if we strive mightily to cooperate with and in grace-filled activity,

then

- we will be filled with grace.

Both Aristotle and Durant would approve of that syllogism, I'm sure. But Aristotle adds a caution: "it is not one swallow or one fine day that makes a spring, so it is not one day or a short time that makes a man blessed and happy." Could St. Bernard have been reading *Nicomachean Ethics* when he opined, "It is not enough to live entirely for Christ. One must have done it for a long time"?

And did you think that Shakespeare must have been the one who observed about one swallow not making a spring?

Note

1. Will Durant, *The Story of Philosophy: The Lives and Opinions of the World's Greatest Philosophers* (New York: Simon & Schuster, 2006), 98.

What Does Hope Look Like?

Tyreke raised his hand one Wednesday at Caldwell College in New Jersey; we were considering individual responsibility, use of the gifts God gives, and how developing one's gifts may be difficult, even seemingly impossible. We spoke of the forces that oppress others, the affronts to human dignity from which many in our society and in that classroom suffered.

Tyreke, a bright fellow with a background filled with challenge, was clearly capable of completing college, though his high school preparation had not been good. He was a pioneer, the first in his family to attempt college. He did not grow up in privilege or in comfort, but had a clear vision of today's struggle preparing for tomorrow's triumph.

He asked, "How do you give hope to those who have no hope?" That stunned me for a moment; I felt that in Tyreke's presence I was in the presence of hope. That virtue was at work restructuring our classroom, our college, and promising to transform the face of the earth. Tyreke was a picture of hope. Next to him was Tyrone, son of a Haitian father and Dominican mother, weary of conflict and poverty, eager to learn and for change. In front of them was Rachel, born in Paterson, a single mother of two while still a teenager, no stranger to suffering or want. Commuting by bus from the Newark projects, Rachel reported that she had been poor long enough; tomorrow would be better.

"How do you give hope to those who have no hope?" Those students are today's gift, and tomorrow's hope. They wondered how to give hope to their contemporaries. Perhaps they were not yet fully aware of their own status as models of hope. They were discovering that their insight, their promise, their hard work, their understanding of the odds and the difficulties were forces that did not weigh them down, but bore them up.

Some students elected Caldwell, a Catholic college in the Dominican tradition, as their first choice among colleges. Others were there because circumstances led them there. But because students, sisters, faculty, and administration and staff are there, God is there, human dignity is there, hope is there. Diligent study, eager socialization, friendly smiles, and warm encounters are all human evidence of divine presence: God is attentive to us, and works in and through us to transform the face of the earth. The students I mention are a picture, I think, of the promise made to Jeremiah in the day of its fulfillment: "I will place my law within them, and write it upon their hearts; I will be their God, and they shall be my people" (Jer 31:33). For thus says the Lord, "See, I am doing something new! / Now it springs forth, do you not perceive it? / In the wilderness I make a way, / in the wasteland, rivers. . . . For I put water in the wilderness / and rivers in the wasteland / for my chosen people to drink" (Isa 43:19-20).

So, "How do you give hope to those who have no hope?" Saint Paul had the answer: "continue [our] pursuit toward the goal, the prize of God's upward calling, in Christ Jesus" (Phil 3:14). Our human labors suggest that the reign of God is in our midst, and we who struggle nobly are signs of hope for those who will be attentive.

The struggle will be neither easy nor brief. So we look for models who demonstrate that the wonders of God are not confined to a distant age or a small group. The wonders of God are seen equally in our age. Tyreke and Rachel and Tyrone live for me as unmistakable signs that the Spirit of God is still at work, in individual hearts, transforming us, revivifying the tired earth.

They are the embodied presence of God's good grace, the Spirit's intriguing promise. They are the future, reminding us that in our efforts, the kingdom of God touches the earth. And then we hear the voice of Jesus: "Whoever serves me must follow me, and where I am, there also will my servant be" (John 12:26).

We will continue to witness to this hope, confident that we will become ever more and more fully what we already are: children of God, known by name and whose very hairs are numbered. We are confident that Jesus, "lifted up from the earth" on the throne of his cross, "will draw everyone" to himself (John 12:33).

When we gather around book and table, we are in the presence of God's good grace. There is the Spirit's intriguing promise. There does the reign of God kiss the earth. We who have lived in the shadows of Lent and renewed our baptismal promises at Easter are the very face of hope because we trust in God's compassion, and in human goodness, and in our own dignity.

What Does Justice Look like from Down There, Shorty?

> For the judgment is merciless to one who has not shown mercy.
> — James 2:13

One day in a rapid-paced discussion of equality and diversity in a university classroom, I noted that college graduates could expect to earn about a million dollars more, over the course of a career, than might their high school classmates who did not pursue higher education. The students, hearing this, registered looks of pleasure. Young Brian jubilantly pumped his right fist in the air. I next noted that men might expect to earn more than women. Brian gave a mocking look of condescending pity to his female classmates.

Next, I said that white men might expect to earn more than men of color. Brian smirked as he turned to his black friend on his right.

Lastly, I said, tall men might expect to earn more than shorter men. "Hey, that's not fair!" Brian immediately and indignantly exclaimed. "Why not?" I asked. "Because I am not very tall," Brian said, whining. Brian described himself as "not very tall." Others of us might have said simply, "short."

No lecture on equality, justice, vision, or fairness could have pointed out the selfishness of his illogical approach better than the good-natured hoots of laughter from all his classmates.

What if the Occupy Movement Had Become a Moveable Feast?

In a rich (well, I think it rich) history of provoking thoughtful worshipers (for better or worse, intentionally and un-), I have never received a louder, longer storm of protest, worried consultations, angry calls, and combative e-mails than when I said in a homily at the height of the 2011 Occupy movement, "A reasonable person might conclude that the work of the church is closely linked to the concerns of the Occupy protesters." Part of the breadth and depth of the reaction was, no doubt, that I said that or something similar in three different homilies in three different places over three long weeks. But still.

Most people of goodwill agree that there is deep inequity in our economic system. One response to that inequity was the Occupy Wall Street protest that spread to other places across the country, including Duluth. One point of the protest was to express frustration about the economy and the hardships many endure, and dismay and disgust over the charge that America's richest four hundred people have more than the nation's bottom 50 percent. And even if this estimate of Michael Moore's cannot be proven to be accurate, this is true: many feared then and fear now that the middle class is rapidly disappearing and soon we will be a nation comprised of the very rich and the very poor.

Christian people who worshiped Sunday by Sunday in the last weeks of the church year and in Advent heard Scriptures proclaimed that might have sensitized them to the plight of those who are less fortunate, and to the concerns of those who call out about injustice. We Christians who follow the common Lectionary, the book of Scripture readings appointed for Sundays throughout the year, have heard on recent Sundays three parables that urge us to faithfulness as we wait in joyful hope for the Messiah to come again. We, with the disciples of Jesus in every age, are called to live in trust, and to recognize that God's love is equitable; this belief makes disciples bold to work for justice as we await the Messiah's return.

The Advent season ought to remind us believers that the God once born among us came to bring reconciliation and peace not apart from the world but in the world. We believe that his light conquers darkness, so we follow eagerly in a world that we experience all at once as both wondrous and vulgar, a world containing both sin and delight.

The Scriptures that the church appoints for the Advent season move us to be alert, to be aware and wary. We hear Jesus in Mark's gospel call us, "Be watchful! Be alert! You do not know when the time will come" (13:33). The apostle Paul asserts that as we wait for the revelation of our Lord Jesus Christ, he will keep us "firm to the end, irreproachable on the day of our Lord Jesus Christ" (1 Cor 1:8).

The call is to the peaceable kingdom, which Isaiah the prophet envisioned, when swords would be beaten into plowshares and spears into pruning hooks. Isaiah's call can be profitably pondered in the garden of the United Nations headquarters in New York City as one considers *Let Us Beat Swords into Plowshares*, a sculpture by Evgeniy Vuchetich, a gift from the then Soviet Union presented in 1959. The sculpted bronze figure of a firmly muscled man holds a hammer in his left hand and a sword in his right that he forms into a plowshare. Thus a tool of war becomes an implement that will work to feed humankind. Isaiah fuels our hopeful attitude, telling us how to prepare to meet the Messiah in making his prayer: "Would that you might meet us doing right, / that we might be mindful of you in our ways!" (64:4).

That Advent sense of introspection and readiness invites us to wonder, what if the Occupy protesters would move from chilly federal plazas to the relative warmth of cathedrals and other worship spaces? Such a move would make sense for a number of reasons: churches tend to be warm; we regard them as holy places; and, not unimportantly, they have flush toilets. The angriest of my interlocutors focused almost exclusively on the toilets. She wanted to bring busloads of people to my college to use our bathrooms. Somehow, she thought, that would teach me a lesson I much needed to learn.

I argued that moral protests have been features of cathedral cultures and courtyards since the Middle Ages. What better place to debate the ethics of capitalism and the social responsibilities of corporations (and congregations too)? Further, church architecture, liturgies, and art are all designed to lift minds and hearts to higher realities. Having glimpsed peace in a holy place or moment, we are then commissioned to go forth glorifying God with our lives, bringing that good news wherever we go.

I was not suggesting that local holy spaces ought to be occupied, but rather pointing out that we ought not be surprised should it have happened. It did happen at St. Paul's Cathedral in London, and so could happen anywhere. Occupying protesters, I thought, could share in the prayer, hear the Scripture proclamations about justice, care for the poor, and love one's enemies.

Even if, as seems now to be the case, the Occupy movement becomes nothing more than a memory, it is a memory that ought to provoke us to ask ourselves what all is involved in truly living what we pray as we begin the preface to the eucharistic prayer. The priest invites, "Let us give thanks to the Lord our God." The people respond, "It is right and just." If in justice we give thanks and praise to God, it follows that we ought to seek to become more and more the people who seek and do, day by day, what is right and just. Jesuit Fr. Pedro Arrupe, once the superior general of the Society of Jesus, reminds us that "if there is hunger anywhere in the world, then our celebration of the Eucharist is somehow incomplete everywhere in the world."[1]

Might a reasonable person then conclude that the work of the church is closely linked to the concerns of the Occupy protesters? All of us envision a new agenda and a just set of priorities. All people of goodwill should be grateful when those concerns are brought to our doorstep. We seek, then, to open our hearts, that by the power of the Spirit, we may be the people Jesus describes: "blessed are those who hear the word of God and observe it" (Luke 11:28). We are both refreshed and nourished by the Eucharist on our journey. In one of the very finest of our prayers after communion (from the Twenty-Seventh Sunday in Ordinary Time), we ask God to grant that we might be transformed into what we consume. Let all the church, the Body of Christ, say, Amen!

That's my story. And I'm sticking to it!

Note

1. Pedro Arrupe, "The Hunger for Bread . . . ," Address to the Forty-first International Eucharistic Congress (Philadelphia, 1976).

Who Can Be Saved?

I preached at my local parish in Chicago at a Sunday evening Mass some years ago; it was a gathering of people from across the city who did not make it to the eucharistic table in the morning. The gospel text was Luke's story of Zacchaeus (19:1-9) in which salvation comes to a wealthy man. I relied on "Hope for the Upwardly Mobile," The Word column from *America* (October 29, 2001) in which John R. Donahue, SJ, insightfully points out that Zacchaeus is revealed as a "true child of Abraham by using his wealth in the service of justice and charity." Jesus the guest brings joy to the house of Zacchaeus, and, as Donahue reads the story, "Zacchaeus is praised not for practicing any particular Christian virtue," but because he is faithful to the covenant with Abraham and to Jewish law in giving alms and making restitution. So, I noted, those who wonder if Jews can be saved have here the words of Jesus himself: "Today salvation has come to this house." Seems sound. It was clear to me that I was not on some dicey theological frontier in making this observation, but simply pointing once more to a familiar Christian truth that ought not to come as a surprise to any Catholic who came of age after the Second Vatican Council.

After the final hymn, standing outside the church and chatting with the worshipers as they left, I was approached by a well-dressed woman who seemed to be in her late thirties. "I am sure I misunderstood you," she said brightly, "but did you say that Jews can be saved?" "Well," said I, "I quoted what Jesus says to Zacchaeus, which seems to make that point." "But he accepted Jesus as his savior," she said. I suggested that she was imposing on the Scripture her own view, which is not found in the text. She continued to press the point that Jews could not win salvation, saying that "our Scriptures and our documents make that clear." I appealed to *lex orandi, lex credendi* ("remember . . . those who take part in this offering, / those gathered here before you, / your entire people, / and all who seek you with a sincere heart," Eucharistic Prayer IV; also, "to whom the Lord our God spoke first," *Roman Missal*, Good Friday 13: General Intercessions, VI) and then to the *Catechism of the Catholic Church* (839, 840, 843, 846, 847). I suggested that she might consult these resources. "You consult them again, because you are incorrect," she said.

She stormed off. My authority as preacher or theologian was as nothing in comparison to what she thought she had been told by the group Jews for Jesus. Or by those cable television mavens who assure angry Catholics that they are always correct and pastors and theologians always suspect. These people, I think, are the poor we will always have with us (Matt 26:11; Mark14:7; John 12:8). Somehow the joy that came to Zacchaeus when he descended from the tree, the joy of which Mary sings in the *Magnificat* (Luke 1:47), and the message of great joy to the shepherds tending their flocks by night (2:10) has escaped them. This fact alone, it seems to me, calls their own orthodoxy into question.

Theology teachers and preachers and pastors assert that God is love and cite Scripture as we do so. But there'll always be someone who insists that God is not really as lenient as our allegedly skewed interpretation of Scripture erroneously suggests. They see God as bound to their tight and unhappy reading of the law, busy chastising those who do not hew to the rigid lines they draw in the incense.

The fact that the God of all graciousness can save all those targeted by divine mercy, inside or outside of the church, is not the real issue here. Simple logic shows that God is bound neither to canon law nor to our stinginess with grace. The issue is pride and prejudice, manners not morals.

Who Is My Neighbor?

How could Moses have been more explicit in what he asked of those who followed him on the long pilgrimage to the Promised Land? He invites them to keep God's "commandments and statutes that are written in this book of the law." Moses suggests, "return to the LORD, your God, with your whole heart and your whole being." Did he ask something beyond their capability? No. He adds, "For this command which I am giving you today is not too wondrous or remote for you." Not too remote or distant at all: "No, it is something very near to you, in your mouth and in your heart, to do it" (Deut 30:10, 11, 14).

Jesus may well have been pondering this Mosaic moment and message when he told the story that is so familiar to us: "There was a scholar of the law who stood up to test [Jesus]." He asked, "Teacher, what must I do to inherit eternal life?" (Luke 10:25). Jesus demonstrated his Jewish credentials by reciting part 2 of the Shema, the central prayer of Judaism from the book of Deuteronomy, recited twice daily by observant Jews: "*You shall love the Lord, your God, with all your heart, with all your being, with all your strength, and with all your mind . . .*" Jesus may or may not have surprised his questioner when he added a second commandment to the first: "*and your neighbor as yourself.*" The questioner could not have known who it was that he questioned. Because, "He replied to [Jesus], 'You have answered correctly.'" Imagine not only giving the Lord a quiz, but then grading him on it! Next, "because he wished to justify himself, he said to Jesus, 'And who is my neighbor?'" Jesus answers by telling the tale of a "man [who] fell victim to robbers" (10:27-30).

There are many features in the story that we should note. Consider first: the injured man was not only passed by, but the priest and the Levite both crossed the road when they saw him. No doubt they were on their way to the temple in Jerusalem, and if they had encountered or assisted the bloody victim, they would have been rendered ritually impure, and thus incapable of making the sacrifice as they intended. But then notice that "a Samaritan traveler who came upon him was moved with compassion at the sight" (10:33). Remember that the Samaritans were outsiders. Jews and Samaritans did not speak to each other. But it is a Samaritan heart that is moved with compassion. The young scholar would hardly have considered the Samaritan a neighbor, much less one to be imitated.

Luke, the gospel writer, tells us this tale of the compassionate Samaritan in chapter 10 of his gospel. He clearly wants us to remember his earlier chapter 7 in which Jesus "journeyed to a city called Nain," where "a man who had died was being carried out, the only son of his mother, and she was a widow." Luke notes, "When the Lord saw her, he was moved with pity for her and said to her, 'Do not weep.' He stepped forward and touched the coffin; at this the bearers halted, and he said, 'Young man, I tell you, arise!' The dead man sat up and began to speak, and Jesus gave him to his mother" (7:11-15).

Up to this point, when Luke has referred to Jesus, he calls him Jesus, but beginning with this encounter with the widow, Luke uses the term Lord for Jesus. For Luke, the Lordship of Jesus is revealed in his compassion, when his heart is moved with pity.

What had to astonish those who heard Jesus tell the tale of the compassionate Samaritan is that an outsider, not a priest or a Levite, is the one who first makes his heart like the heart of Jesus. The others may have made it to the temple and performed there the ritual duties assigned to them, but they had missed the opportunity to be people of compassion, people to make their hearts like the heart of Jesus.

Notice next that Jesus quizzes the one who first quizzed him: "Which of these three, in your opinion, was neighbor to the robbers' victim?" The answer is simple: the Samaritan. But instead, the answer came: "The one who treated him with mercy." The speaker avoided even speaking the word Samaritan, the name of the group he despised. But then he is issued a challenge: "Jesus said to him, 'Go and do likewise'" (10:36-37). Imagine the consternation the young scholar must have felt. He is invited to imitate the virtue of the one he had despised. How very many complicating factors this invitation must have introduced into his life and his heart.

The challenge is ours as well: to make our hearts like the heart of Jesus, moved with compassion to act in love.

Window, White Cane, and the Body of Christ

A very old priest in my diocese (may he be with God!) used to delight in telling the story of his seminary classmates being assembled for a school picture many years ago. All of the students stood solemnly in front of the seminary building, wearing their cassocks, while the photographer moved his primitive camera from left to right, slowly, to make one of those long, narrow photographs you sometimes see from days gone by.

Only when the picture was completed, framed, and ready to be hung in the seminary hall was it noticed that clearly visible in an upstairs window was one of the German nuns who had come to the States to care for the seminarians and their priest professors. Newly arrived in America, only able to speak bits of English, the nun appeared in the photo making an obscene gesture. The rector of the seminary asked the naive sister for an explanation and was told, "The boys invited me to be in the picture. They told me that the gesture meant, 'Greetings to the student body.'"

The moral seems to be, be careful what you do or say. And where.

That moral came home to me again resoundingly on my first visit to lovely Honolulu. One day there, I was asked by a priest friend to take his place at daily Eucharist. In the front pew, I noticed a blind man wearing large, dark glasses, with a white cane at his side. I never saw him smile.

Before the Lamb of God, I quoted St. Paul: "This bread that we break, is it not the body of Christ, given for us? . . ."

After Mass, I crossed the parking lot and entered the lobby of the building in which the parish priests lived. Moving toward the elevator, I noticed the blind man from church, glasses on and white cane tapping, making his way into the elevator. With him was a woman who had been the reader at Mass who also lived in the building. She nodded a greeting to me, we entered the elevator together, she punched in his floor and her own.

Just as I was about to speak, the blind man spoke. "Did you hear what that priest told us?" The woman trapped in the elevator with us flashed me a pained look. I realized that he did not know that I too was in the ascending elevator.

"He told us, 'This is not the body of Christ. This is not the blood of Christ.'" I was stunned speechless. The elevator stopped on the fifth floor and he tapped his way out with his white cane.

It seemed striking to me later that the aggressor was blind. What a perfect metaphor his blindness was for the other kind of blindness that can afflict us. Since then, I often wonder what I have failed to see.

Wisdom and Holiness

> Gird your loins and light your lamps
> and be like servants who await their master's return from
>   a wedding,
> ready to open immediately when he comes and knocks.
> —Luke 12:35-36

What does it mean to be wise? We are given a clue to that when someone newly baptized or from the family of the newly baptized lights a candle from the Easter candle for the newest member of the church. What the priest or deacon says then explains perfectly the significance and symbolism of the candle and the gift of light. He admonishes the parents and godparents that the light is entrusted to them to be kept burning brightly. Those baptized have been enlightened by Christ and are to walk always as children of the light. We pray that they keep the flame of faith alive in their hearts so that when the Lord comes, they may go out to meet him with all the saints in the heavenly kingdom.

If we really wish to fully understand what is promised to and expected of us in that ritual moment, we need to go back to the gospel story of the wise and foolish maidens (Matt 25:1-13). The bridegroom in the story is Jesus, and those who wait for his return are members of the church. Those who are alert, whose lamps are burning brightly, are the ones whose deeds prepare them to greet the Lord in joy when at last he will come.

Sometimes people say that the ones with oil should have shared with those whose lamps had burned out. If the oil stands for our good deeds, they are a commodity that cannot be shared with those who have none. We, each of us, are challenged to be ready when the Lord calls. The liturgy of baptism reminds us of the challenge, and the call to wisdom and holiness, that is ours every day of our lives!

Work of Bees

The *Exsultet*, or Easter proclamation, is the hymn of praise sung by the deacon or priest in the presence of the newly blessed paschal candle at the great vigil of Easter. Here the work of bees is remembered and acknowledged: "On this, your night of grace, O holy Father, / accept this candle, a solemn offering, / the work of bees and of your servants' hands, / an evening sacrifice of praise, / this gift from your most holy Church." We sing "the praises of this pillar, / which glowing fire ignites for God's honor, / a fire into many flames divided, / yet never dimmed by sharing of its light, / for it is fed by melting wax, / drawn out by mother bees / to build a torch so precious."

Pius XII addressed the apiarists of Italy in 1948 at their national convention: "Impelled and guided by instinct, a visible trace and testimony of the unseen wisdom of the Creator, what lessons do not bees give to men, who are, or should be, guided by reason, the living reflection of the divine intellect!

"Bees are models of social life and activity, in which each class has its duty to perform and performs it exactly—one is almost tempted to say conscientiously—without envy, without rivalry, in the order and position assigned to each, with care and love. Even the most inexperienced observer of bee culture admires the delicacy and perfection of this work."

Do not the bees and their inclusion in the *Exsultet* invite us, as we praise God, to admire as well the delicacy and perfection of the crafts and arts that assist the church at prayer?

Zed, Z, in Conclusion: Running with the "Inexpressible Delight of Love"

We Christians receive serious butt-kickings from time to time in the opinion pages of my local newspaper. We need and deserve such reminders when we fail in our efforts to live the life of Jesus with hearts moved by compassion. Our failures should not be explained away; that would serve neither church nor larger community.

The Christian Scriptures clearly announce that each member is graced (see 1 Cor 12:13). Yet there is much that is deficient and even un-prophetic in our current efforts, much to be lamented in what we leave undone. There are many moments in our Christian lives when we might certainly wonder how well we understand the absolute nature of human dignity, and how often we sin against that dignity in the treatment that many of God's people endure even in and from the church. The mainline churches are hemorrhaging members; the numbers of our young people are just a shadow of what they were a generation ago.

When St. Benedict concluded the Prologue to his Rule for monasteries, he noted, "But as we progress in this way of life and in faith, we shall run on the path of God's commandments, our hearts overflowing with the inexpressible delight of love. Never swerving from his instructions, then, but faithfully observing his teaching . . . until death, we shall through patience share in the sufferings of Christ that we may deserve also to share in his kingdom. Amen" (49-50). Benedict makes it clear, not just to monastics, but to all seekers of God, that we must be attentive and open to the possibilities that each day brings, for these are the opportunities for us to seek and serve God in ways that, as the Rule points out, are neither harsh nor burdensome. The challenge is to be active and alert, aware always of the holiness that surrounds us, of the divinity to which we aspire.

Michael Casey points out in *The Road to Eternal Life*, "Ultimately, attaining the goal of eternal life is not a triumph of personal achievement; it comes from the closeness of our relationship with Christ.

Entering his kingdom presupposes that we are conformed to him, that our life has become progressively more Christlike."[1]

Thinking about all this, I went for a hike in the skywalk downtown and overheard just a snatch of conversation between two young guys, maybe fifteen years old, one telling another earnestly, "Well, the spirituality I follow . . ." I wondered what spirituality that might be, if it is one he crafts to fit occasions or moods or moments, or if it might be some personalized variant of a religion he has read or heard about. I also wondered why a teenager would think he has to craft a spirituality. What about a ready-made spirituality: maybe Methodism or Catholicism. We who seek to follow Jesus in the company of the church have a spirituality readily at hand, one proven by saints and mystics over all the ages. How about studying the religion that "teaches that God became what we are so we could become what God is?"[2] That's Christianity, of course.

Some will suggest, in fact many will insist, that the church in our age is riddled with bad will and ineffective leadership; that it is increasingly irrelevant in the power struggles that overshadow a true spirit of evangelism, with angry apologetics taking the place of sincere gospel outreach. Whenever I hear a Catholic speak of "telling the truth in love," I cringe; he means something quite different, I am afraid, than does St. Benedict, when he writes about running the way of God's commandments "with the inexpressible delight of love."

When I made this lament recently while preaching at the Basilica in Minneapolis, a fellow observed later that we have in the church a pearl of great price, but we have difficulty seeing and recognizing it, because that pearl is in a bucket of murky water. Those who see only the murky water may have limited vision. If we are responsible in any way for making clear water murky, or murky water darker, then we have failed in our Catholic duty. If we wish to see the face of God, we must prepare ourselves not just to insist on orthodoxy and strict observance of the law as we choose to understand it. That is not enough. It is not even a beginning. Instead, we who hope to save our souls and to see the face of God must do exactly as St. Benedict wrote and advised all those centuries ago: We must let our hearts expand, that we might "run on the path of God's commandments, our hearts overflowing with the inexpressible delight of love. Never swerving from his instructions, then, but faithfully observing his teaching . . . until death, we shall through patience share in the sufferings of Christ that we may deserve also to share in his kingdom" (Prol. 49-50). Amen!

Notes

1. Michael Casey, *The Road to Eternal Life: Reflections on the Prologue of Benedict's Rule* (Collegeville, MN: Liturgical Press, 2011), 179.

2. Richard G. Malloy, "Religious Life in the Age of Facebook: Where have all the young people gone?" *America* 199, no. 1 (July 7, 2008).

www.ingramcontent.com/pod-product-compliance
Lightning Source LLC
Chambersburg PA
CBHW071923290426
44110CB00013B/1452